JF

Cinderella III : a twist in
 time

Walt Disney Pictures Presents

Cinderella III

A Twist In Time

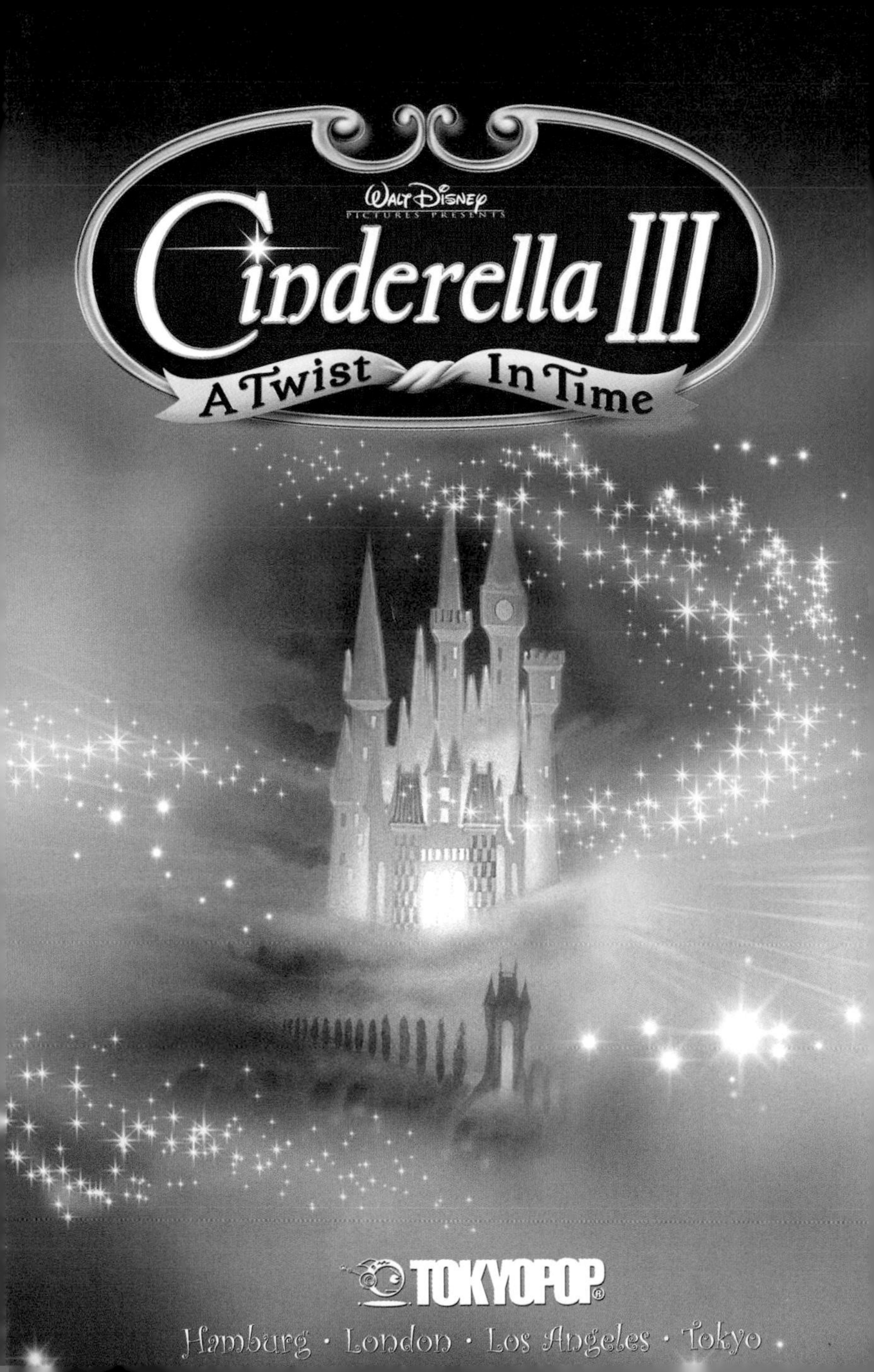

TOKYOPOP

Hamburg · London · Los Angeles · Tokyo

Editor - Julie Taylor
Contributing Editors - Amy Court Kaemon
Graphic Designer and Letterer - Anna Kernbaum
Cover Designer & Graphic Artist - Monalisa J. de Asis

Production Manager - Elisabeth Brizzi
Art Director - Anne Marie Horne
VP of Production - Ron Klamert
Editor in Chief - Rob Tokar
Publisher - Mike Kiley
President & C.O.O. - John Parker
C.E.O. & Chief Creative Officer - Stuart Levy

E-mail: info@TOKYOPOP.com
Come visit us online at www.TOKYOPOP.com

A **TOKYOPOP** Cine-Manga® Book
TOKYOPOP Inc.
5900 Wilshire Blvd., Suite 2000
Los Angeles, CA 90036

Cinderella III

ISBN: 978-1-59816-912-6

First TOKYOPOP® printing: February 2007

10 9 8 7 6 5 4 3 2 1

Printed in the USA

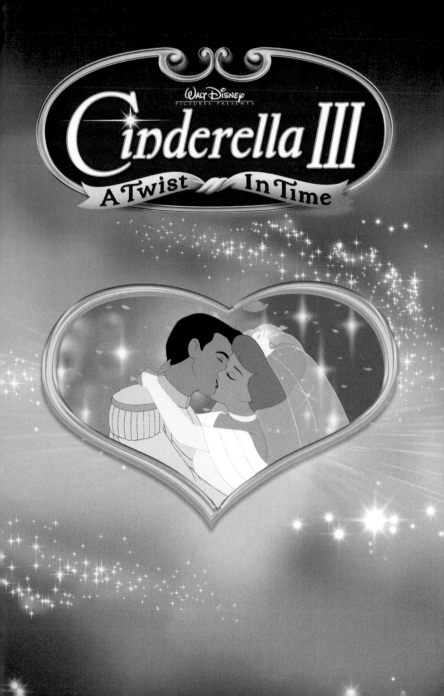

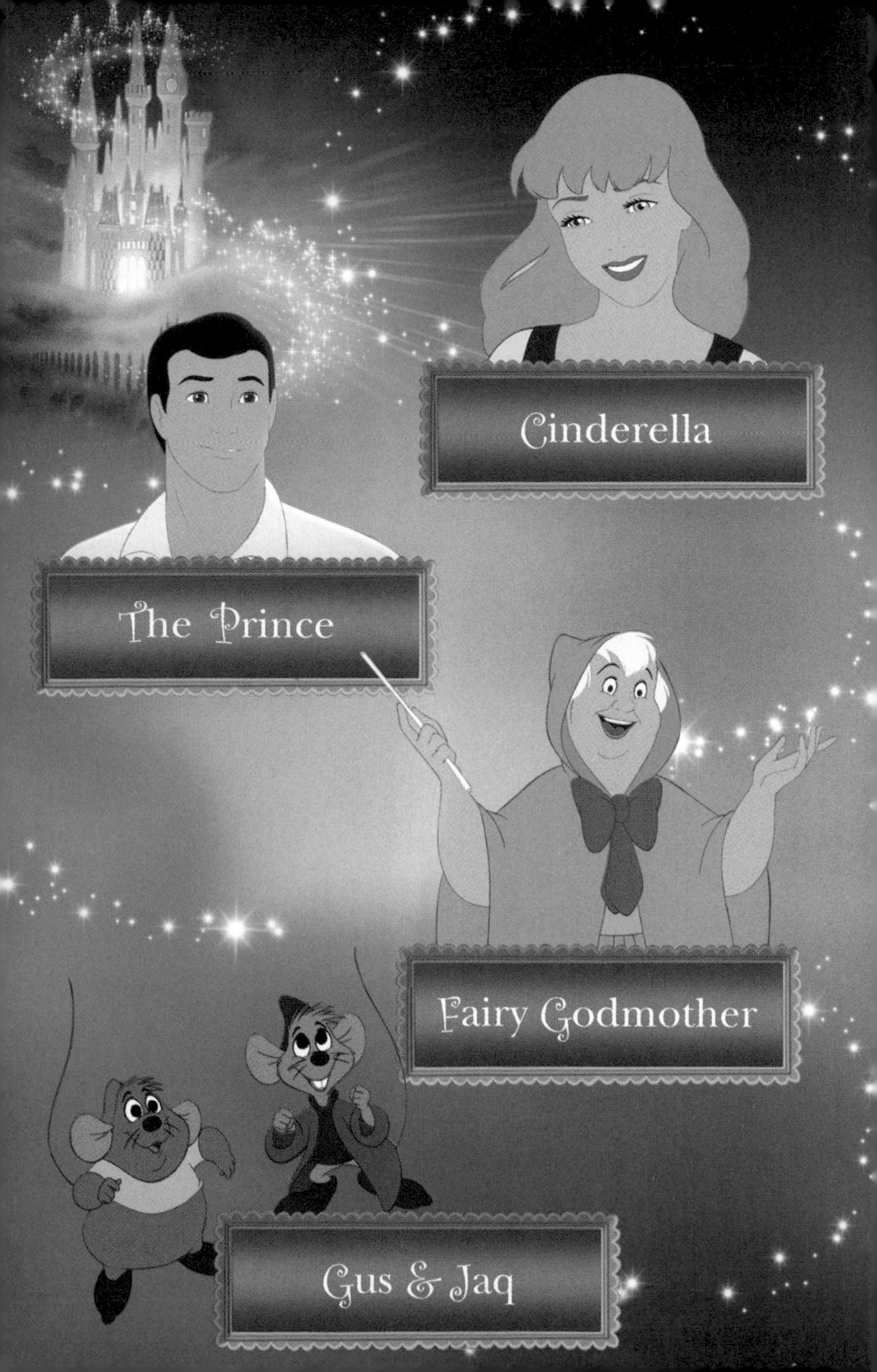
Cinderella
The Prince
Fairy Godmother
Gus & Jaq

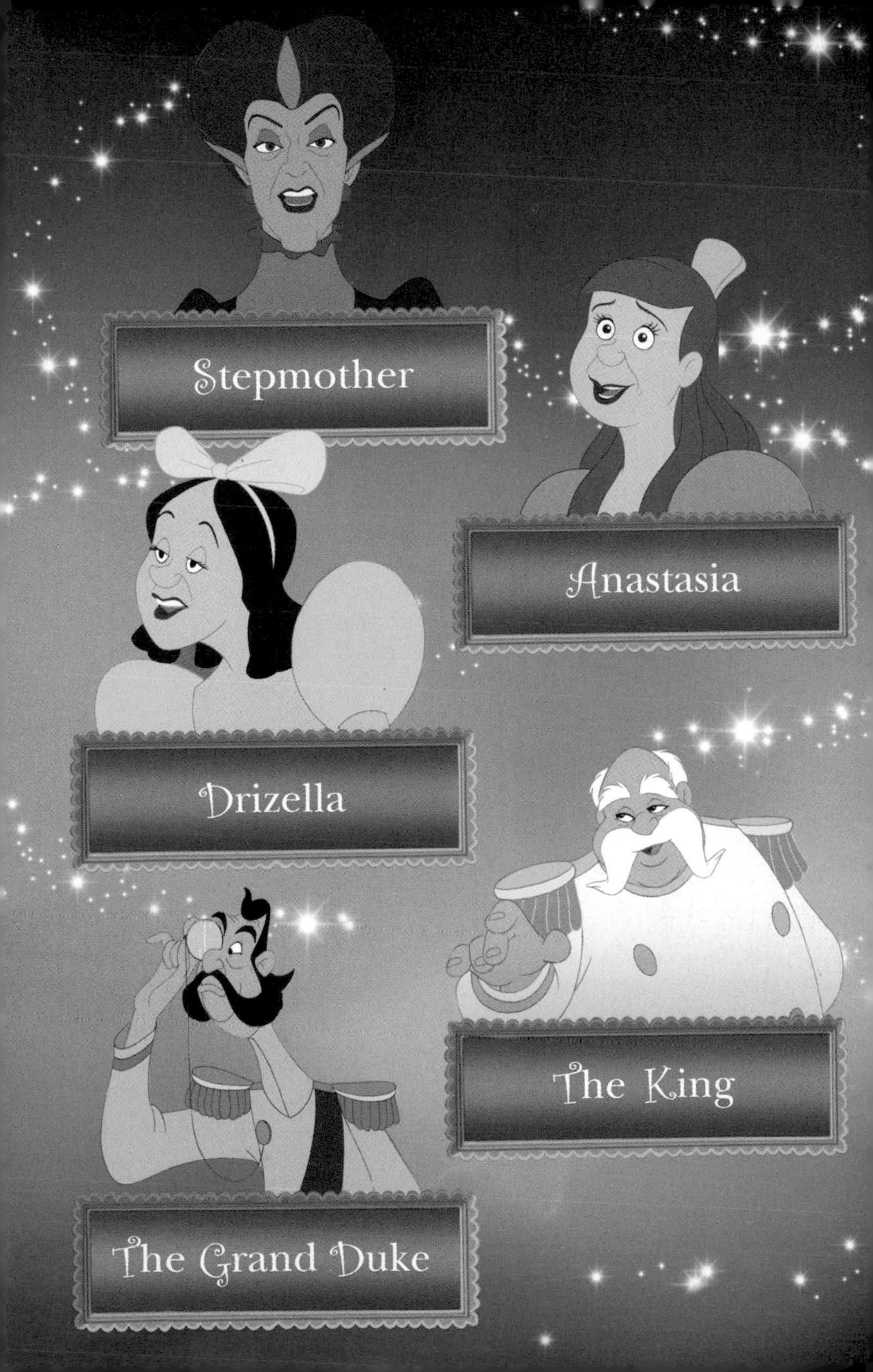
Stepmother
Anastasia
Drizella
The King
The Grand Duke

Once upon a time, exactly one year after a fairy tale wedding...
Do you remember the story of a girl who found true love because she kept a beautiful dream in her heart?
Well, that girl is me.
Better hurry. Fairy Godmother's waiting.

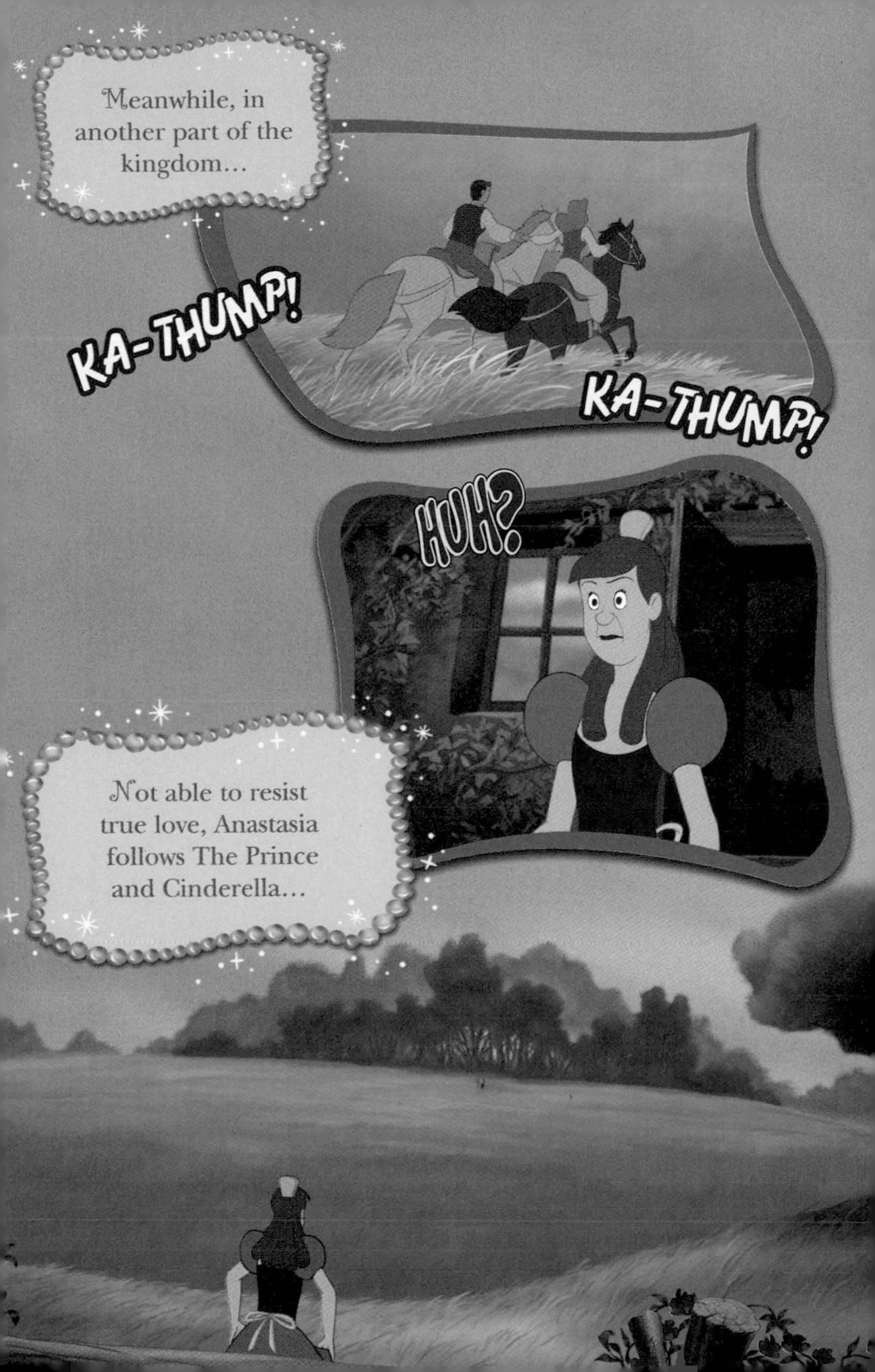
Meanwhile, in another part of the kingdom...
KA-THUMP!
KA-THUMP!
HUH?
Not able to resist true love, Anastasia follows The Prince and Cinderella...

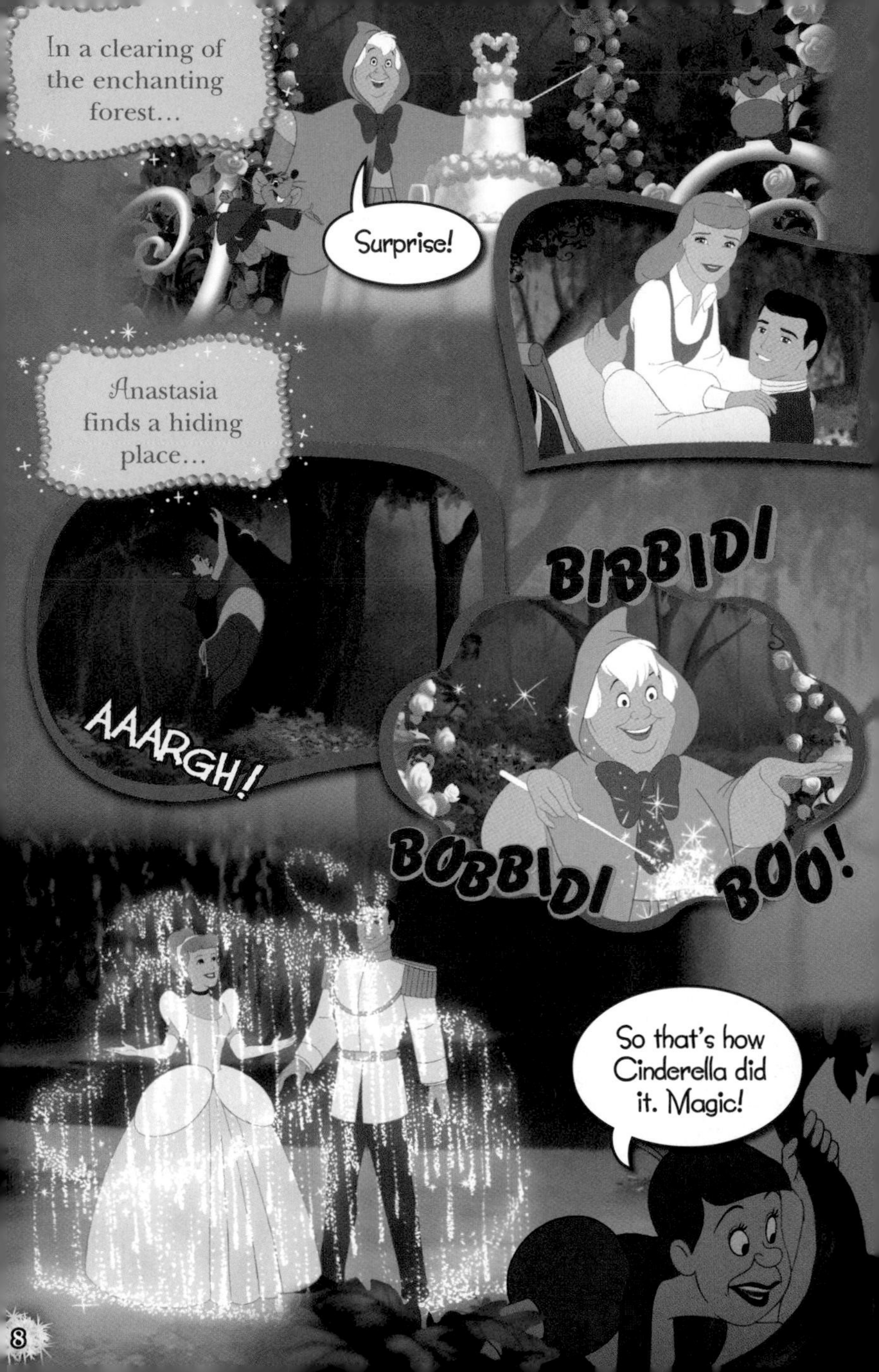
In a clearing of the enchanting forest...
Surprise!
Anastasia finds a hiding place...
AAARGH!
BIBBIDI
BOBBIDI
BOO!
So that's how Cinderella did it. Magic!

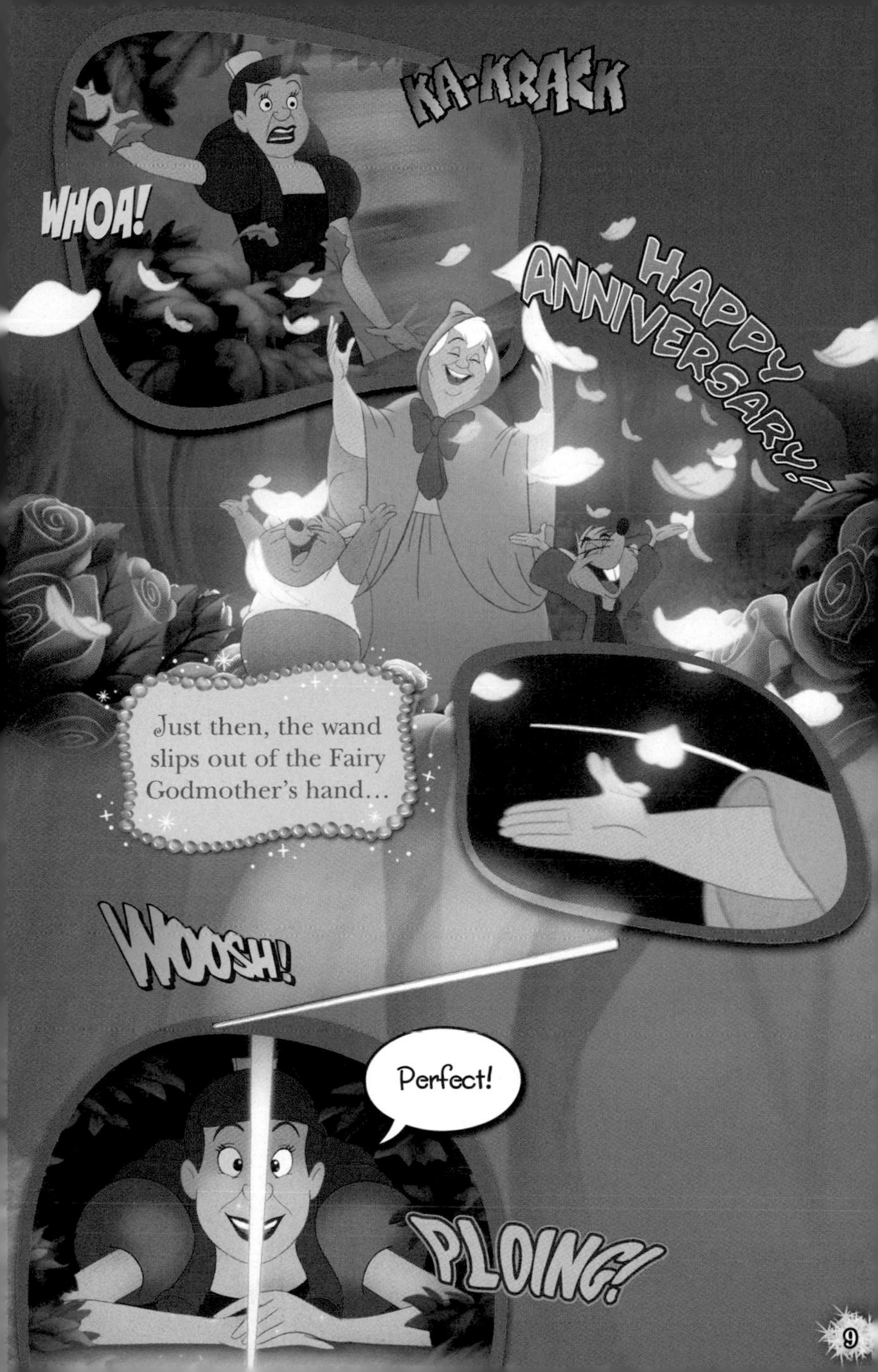
KA-KRACK
WHOA!
HAPPY ANNIVERSARY!
Just then, the wand slips out of the Fairy Godmother's hand…
WHOOSH!
Perfect!
PLOING!

Anastasia returns home with the wand...
...with the Fairy Godmother close at her heels.
Mother, our troubles are over!
Child, put that down. That wand could be extremely dangerous.
I need it, you silly old garden gnome! Bibbidi-bobbidi-boo!
KZZZZZZASH!
The Fairy Godmother is turned into a garden statue!

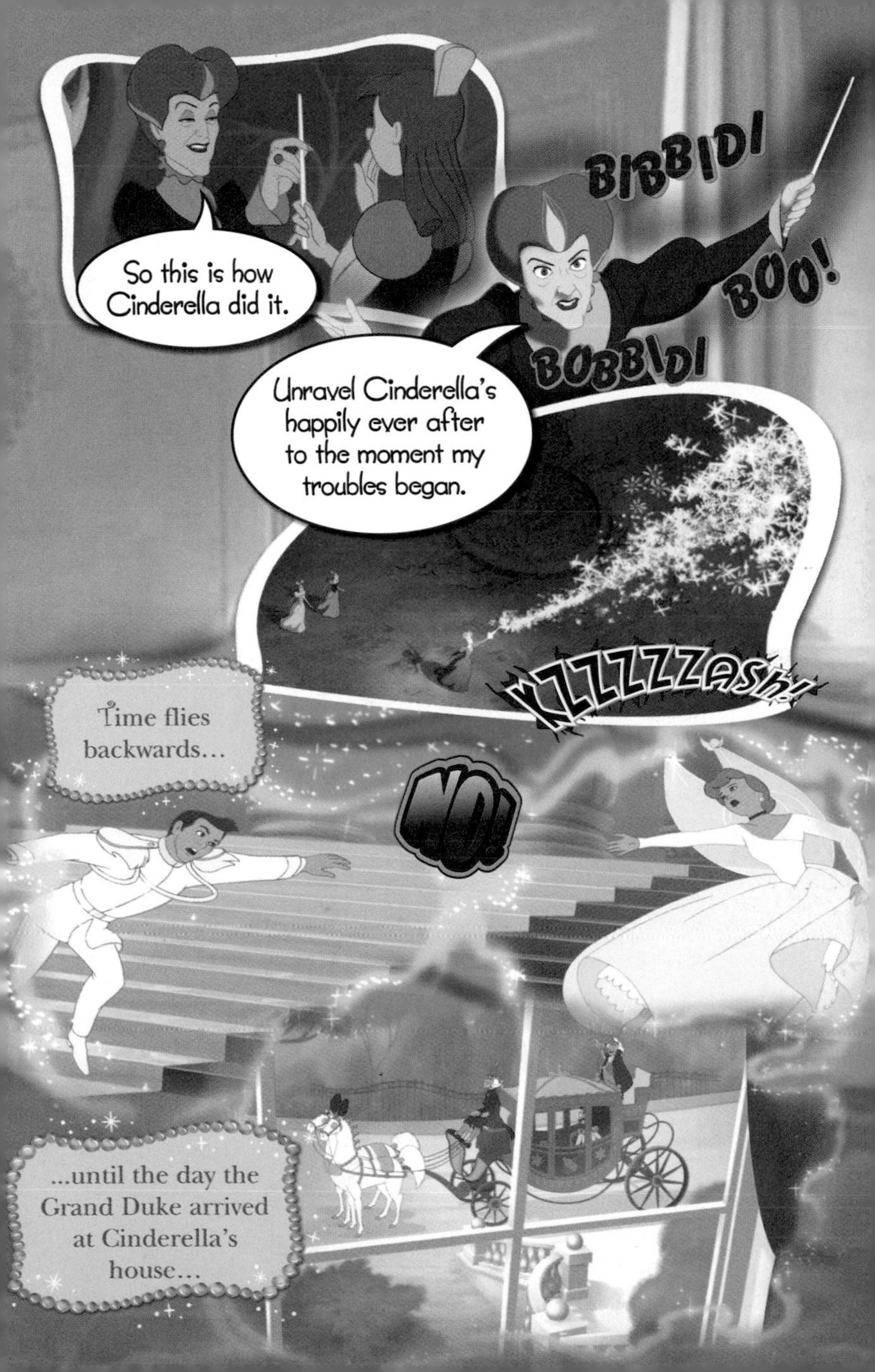
So this is how Cinderella did it.
BIBBIDI
BOBBIDI
BOO!
Unravel Cinderella's happily ever after to the moment my troubles began.
KZZZZZZash!
Time flies backwards...
NO!
...until the day the Grand Duke arrived at Cinderella's house...

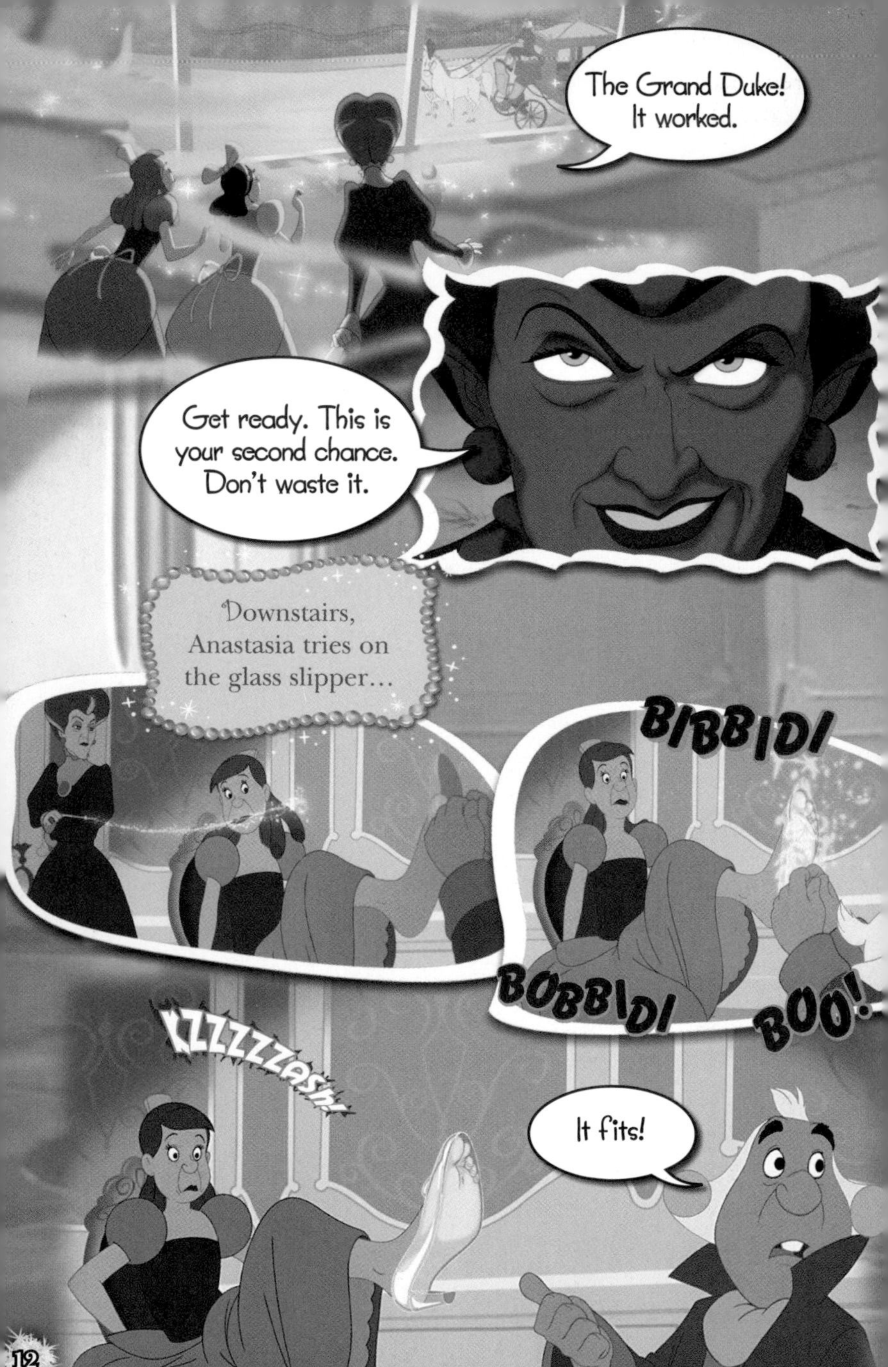
The Grand Duke!
It worked.
Get ready. This is
your second chance.
Don't waste it.
Downstairs,
Anastasia tries on
the glass slipper...
BIBBIDI
BOBBIDI
BOO!
KZZZZZZASH!
It fits!

I hereby declare that we have found the Prince's bride-to-be.
From the top of the staircase...
I danced with the Prince. That was my slipper.
The slipper fits Anastasia. And that's who he's marrying.
Stay away from the palace. Stay away from the Prince.
KLINK!
And with that, the wicked Stepmother flings Cinderella's slipper to the floor...
KRACK

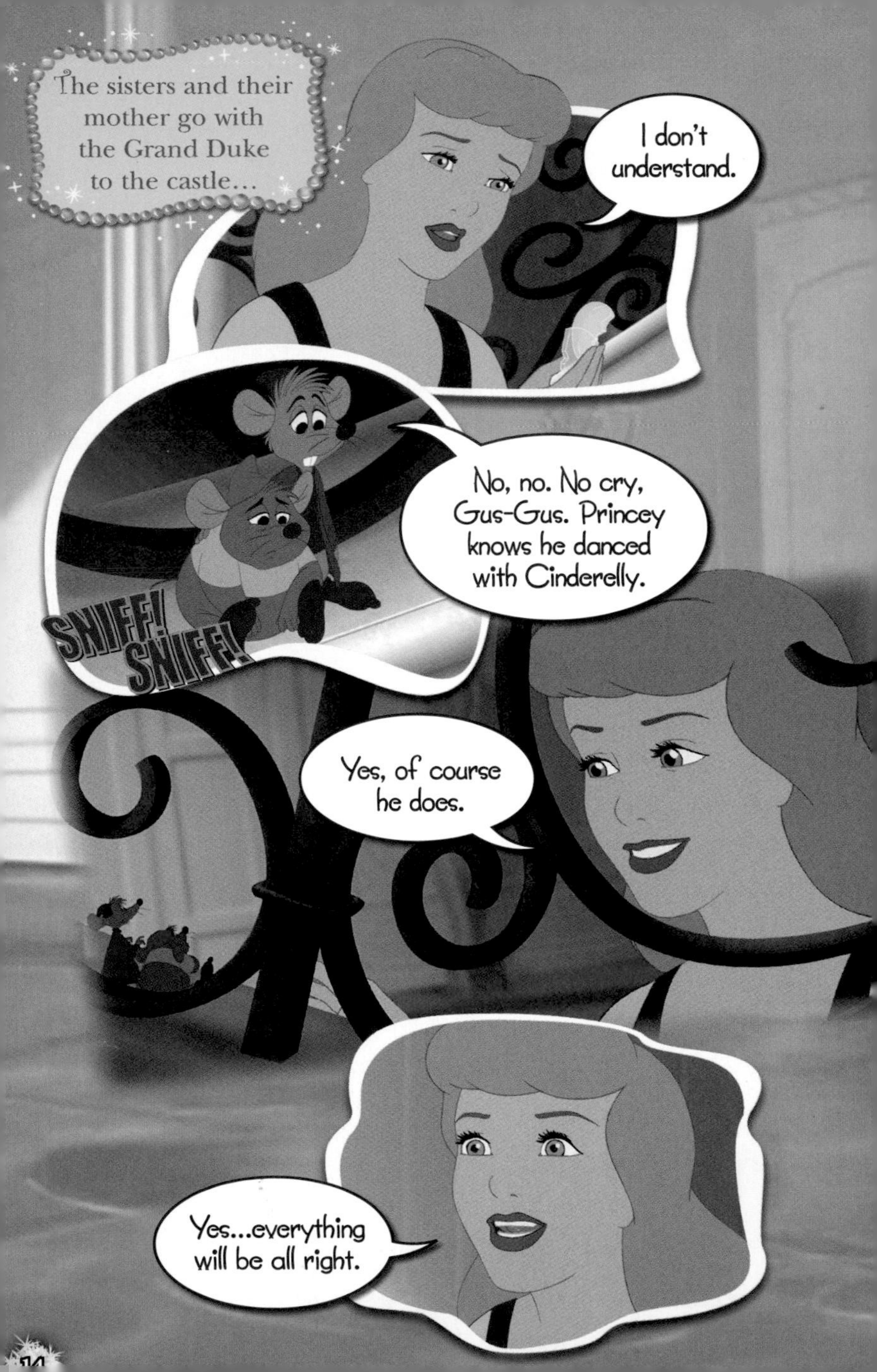
The sisters and their mother go with the Grand Duke to the castle...
I don't understand.
No, no. No cry, Gus-Gus. Princey knows he danced with Cinderelly.
SNIFF! SNIFF!
Yes, of course he does.
Yes...everything will be all right.

At the castle, the Prince rushes to meet his bride-to-be…
They've found her!
My Prince!
There...there seems to be a little mix-up here.
But with the wand in her possession…
You will forget who you danced with and marry the girl who fits the slipper. Tonight.
BIBBIDI
BOBBIDI
BOO!

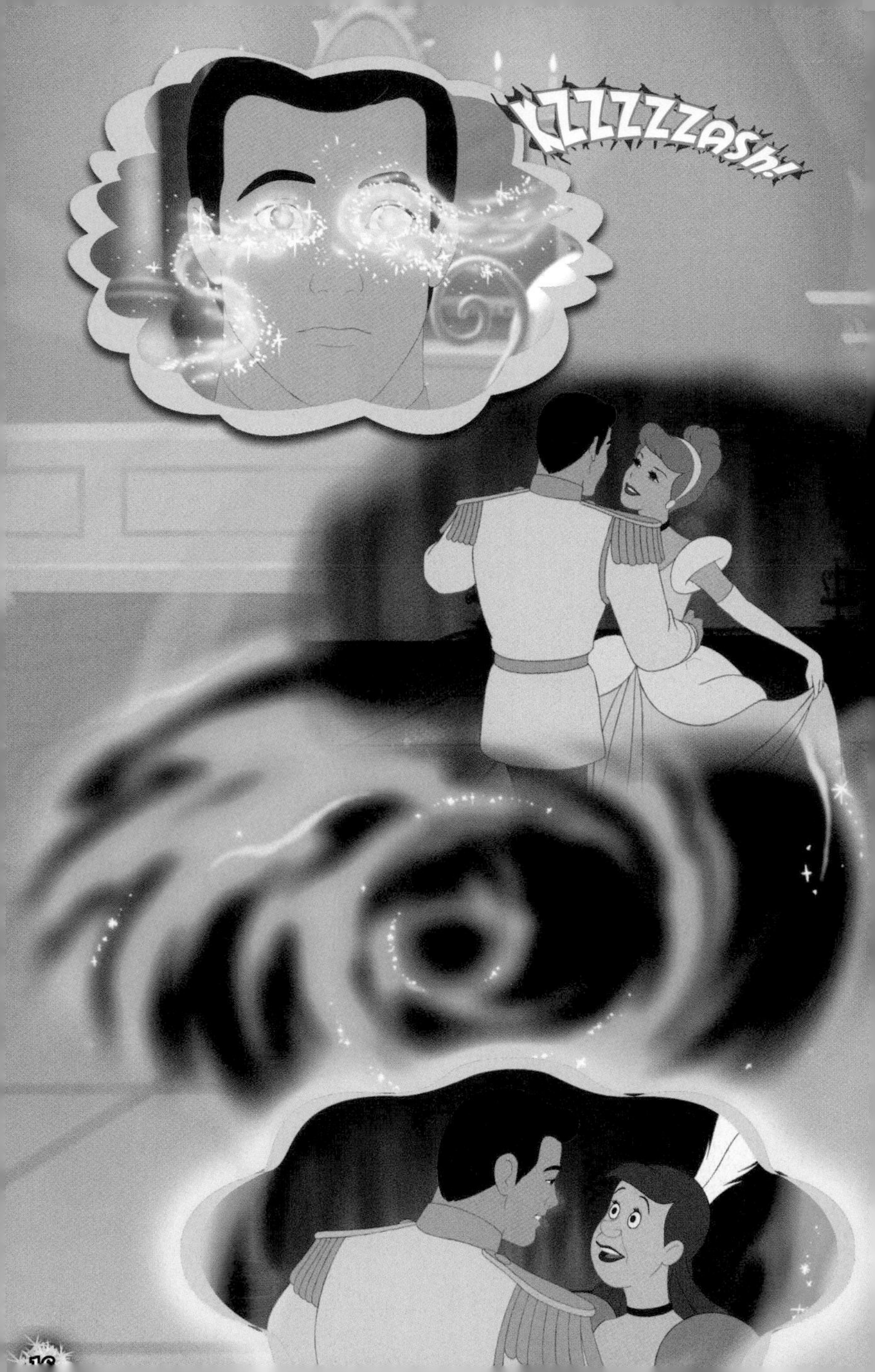
KZZZZZASH!

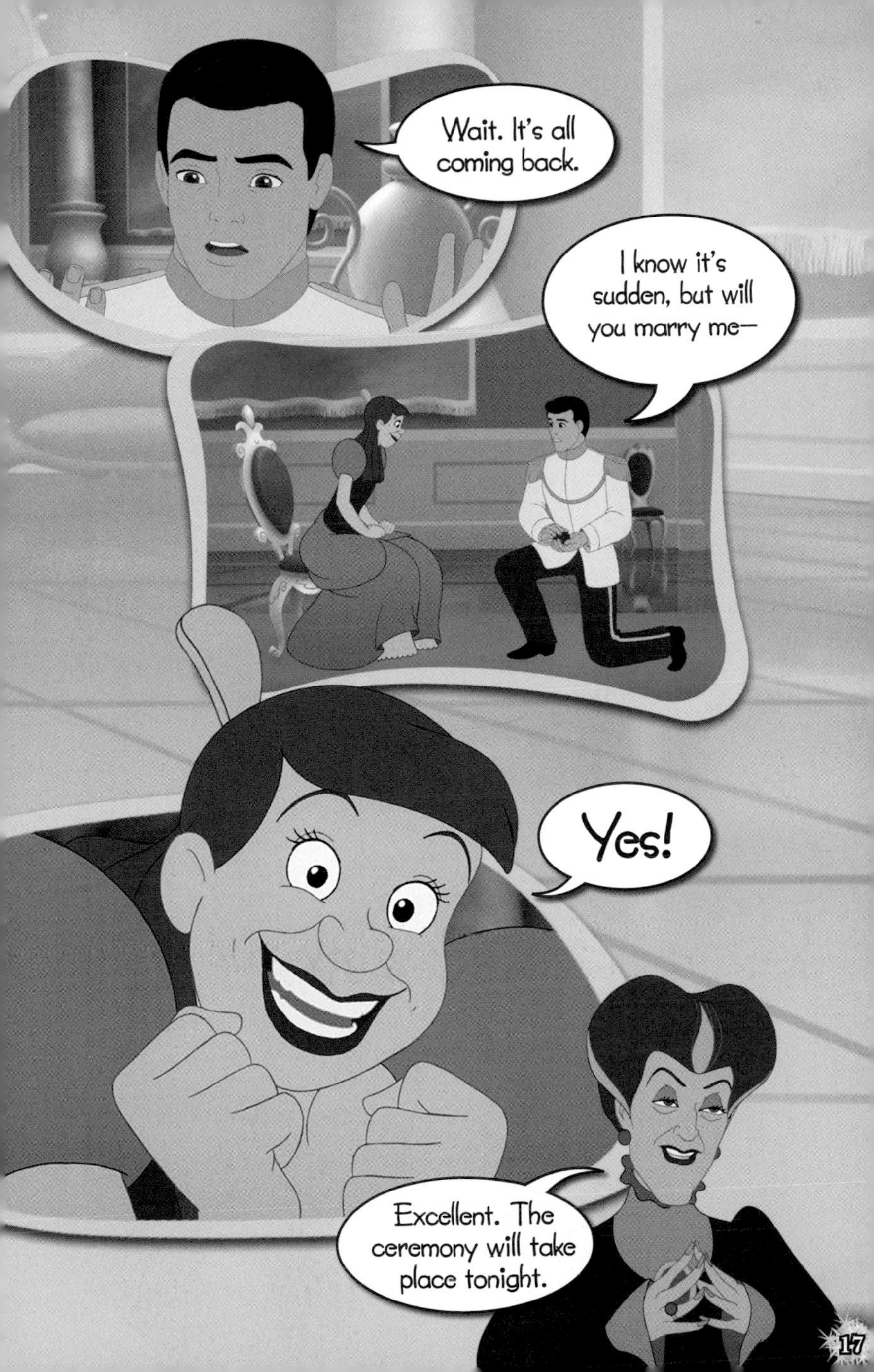
Wait. It's all coming back.
I know it's sudden, but will you marry me—
Yes!
Excellent. The ceremony will take place tonight.

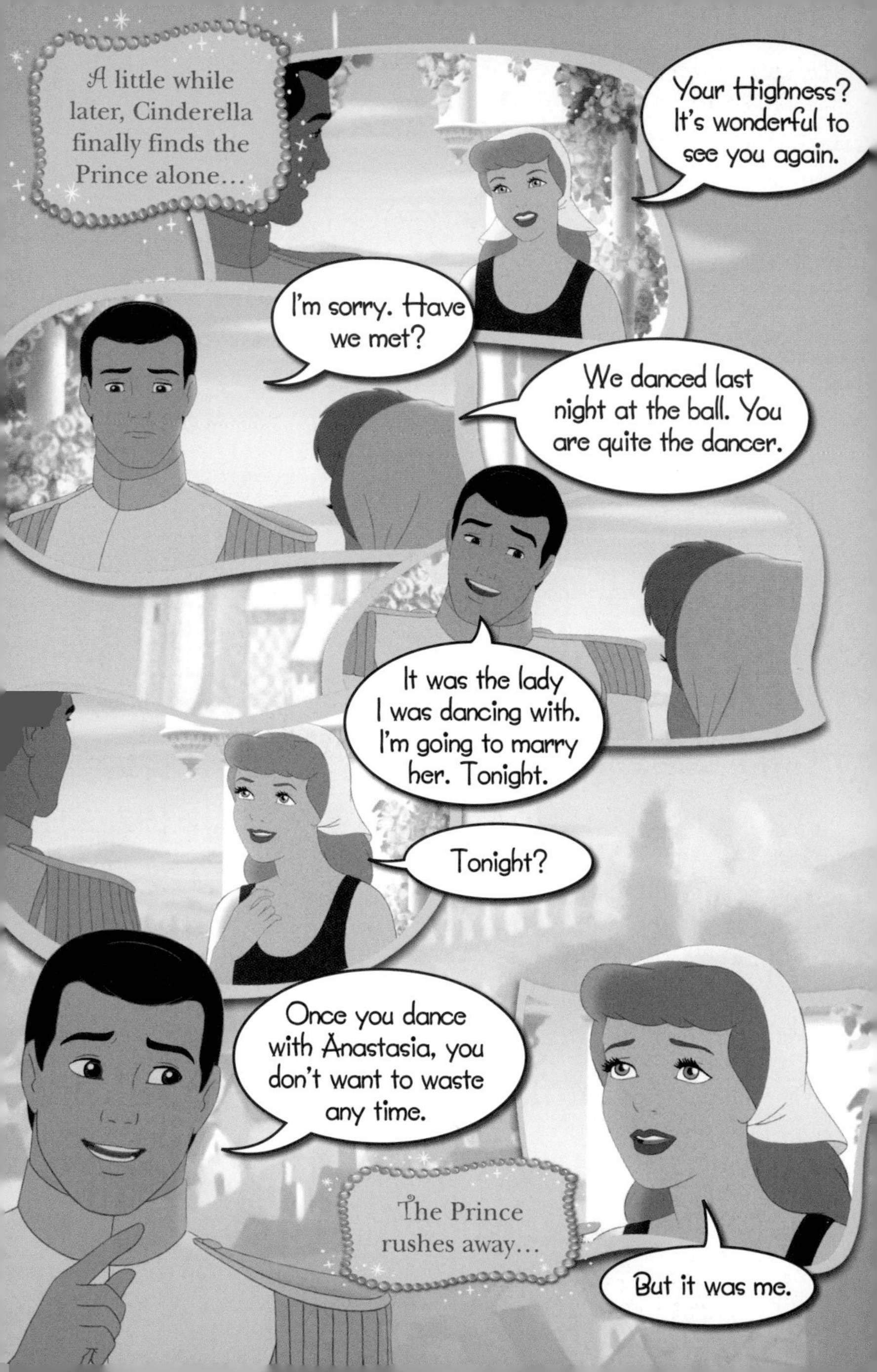
A little while later, Cinderella finally finds the Prince alone…
Your Highness? It's wonderful to see you again.
I'm sorry. Have we met?
We danced last night at the ball. You are quite the dancer.
It was the lady I was dancing with. I'm going to marry her. Tonight.
Tonight?
Once you dance with Anastasia, you don't want to waste any time.
The Prince rushes away…
But it was me.

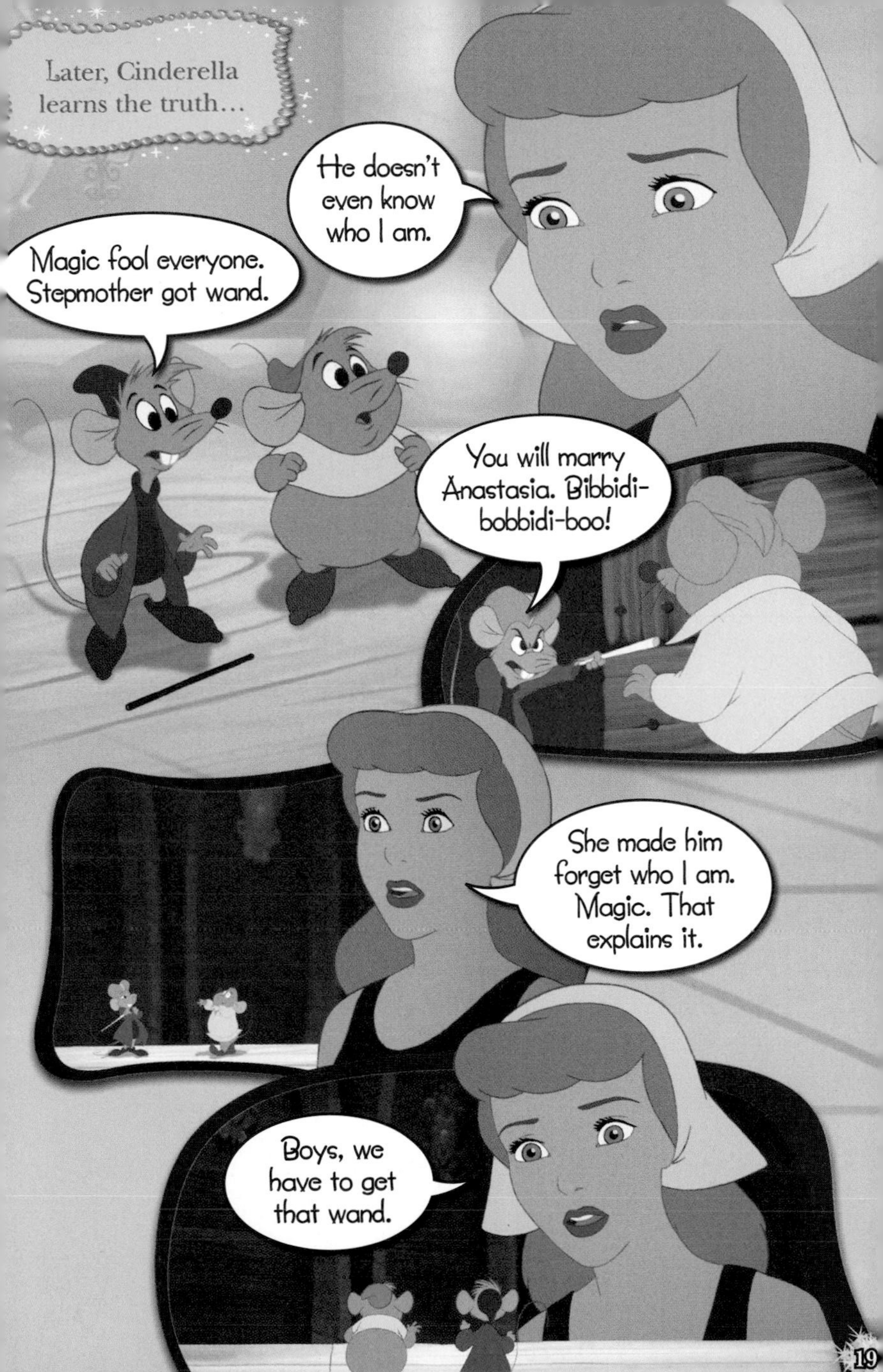
Later, Cinderella learns the truth…
He doesn't even know who I am.
Magic fool everyone. Stepmother got wand.
You will marry Anastasia. Bibbidi-bobbidi-boo!
She made him forget who I am. Magic. That explains it.
Boys, we have to get that wand.

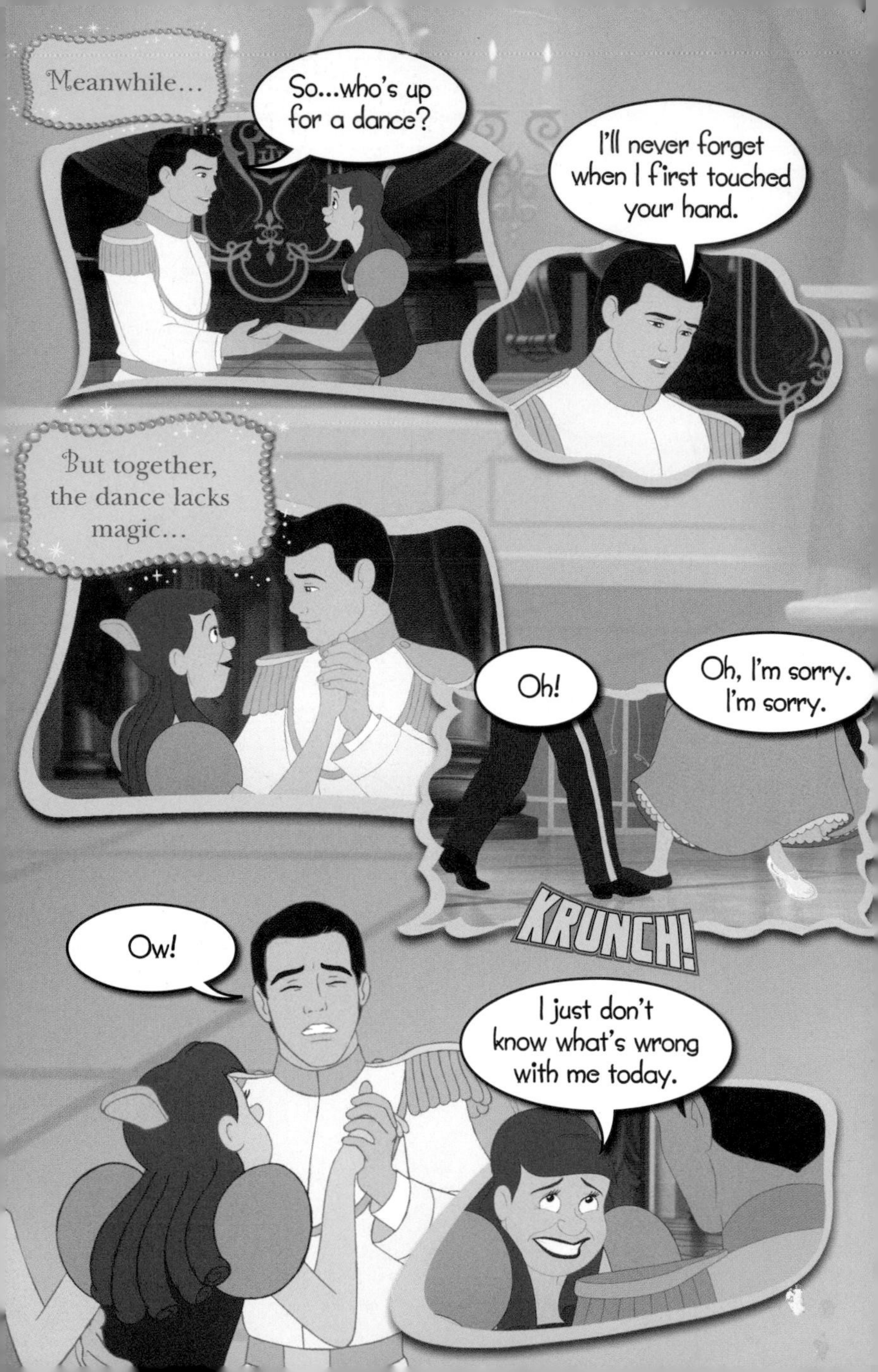
Meanwhile...
So...who's up for a dance?
I'll never forget when I first touched your hand.
But together, the dance lacks magic...
Oh!
Oh, I'm sorry. I'm sorry.
KRUNCH!
Ow!
I just don't know what's wrong with me today.

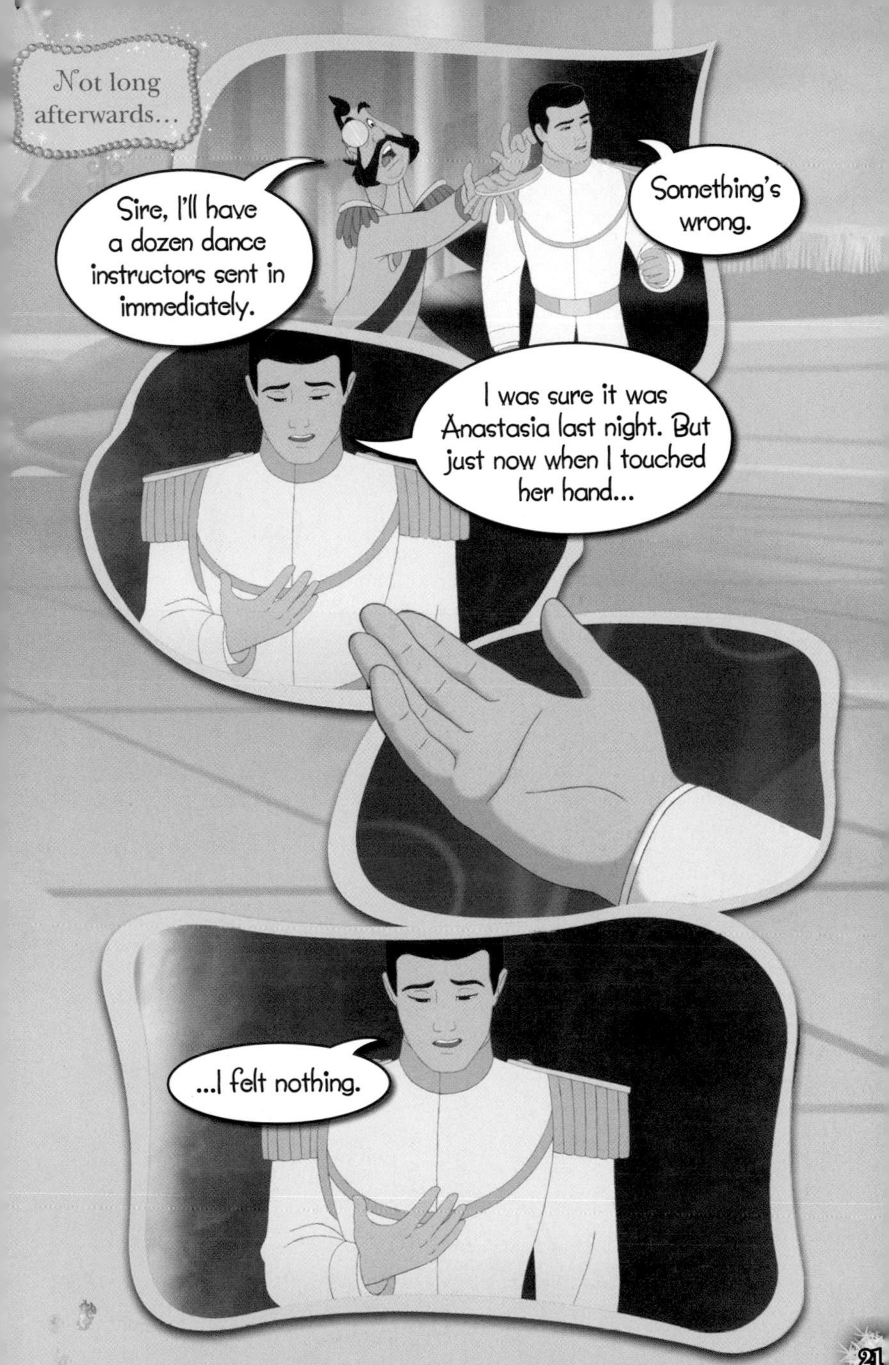
Not long afterwards...
Sire, I'll have a dozen dance instructors sent in immediately.
Something's wrong.
I was sure it was Anastasia last night. But just now when I touched her hand...
...I felt nothing.

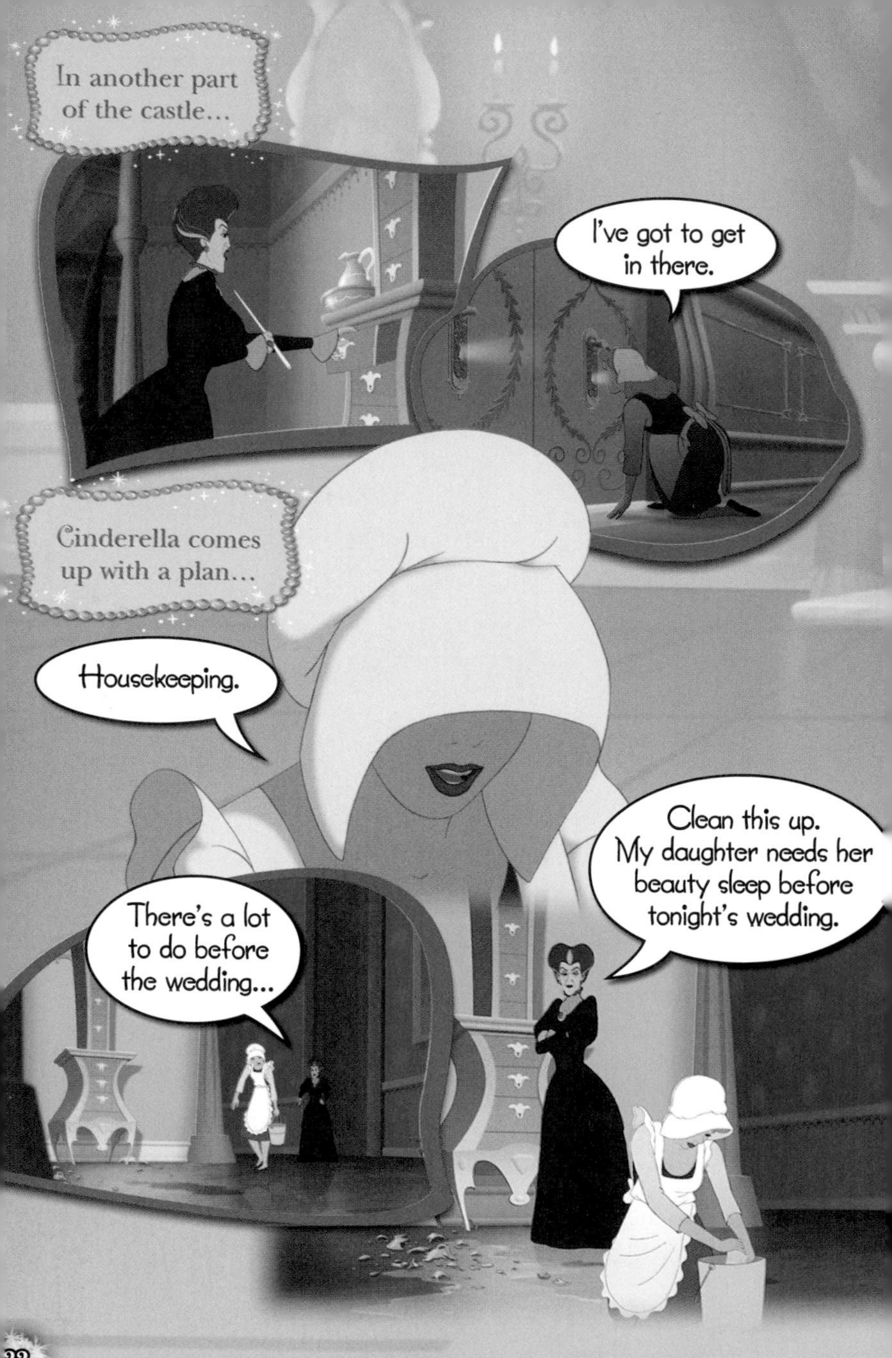

In another part of the castle...
I've got to get in there.
Cinderella comes up with a plan...
Housekeeping.
There's a lot to do before the wedding...
Clean this up. My daughter needs her beauty sleep before tonight's wedding.

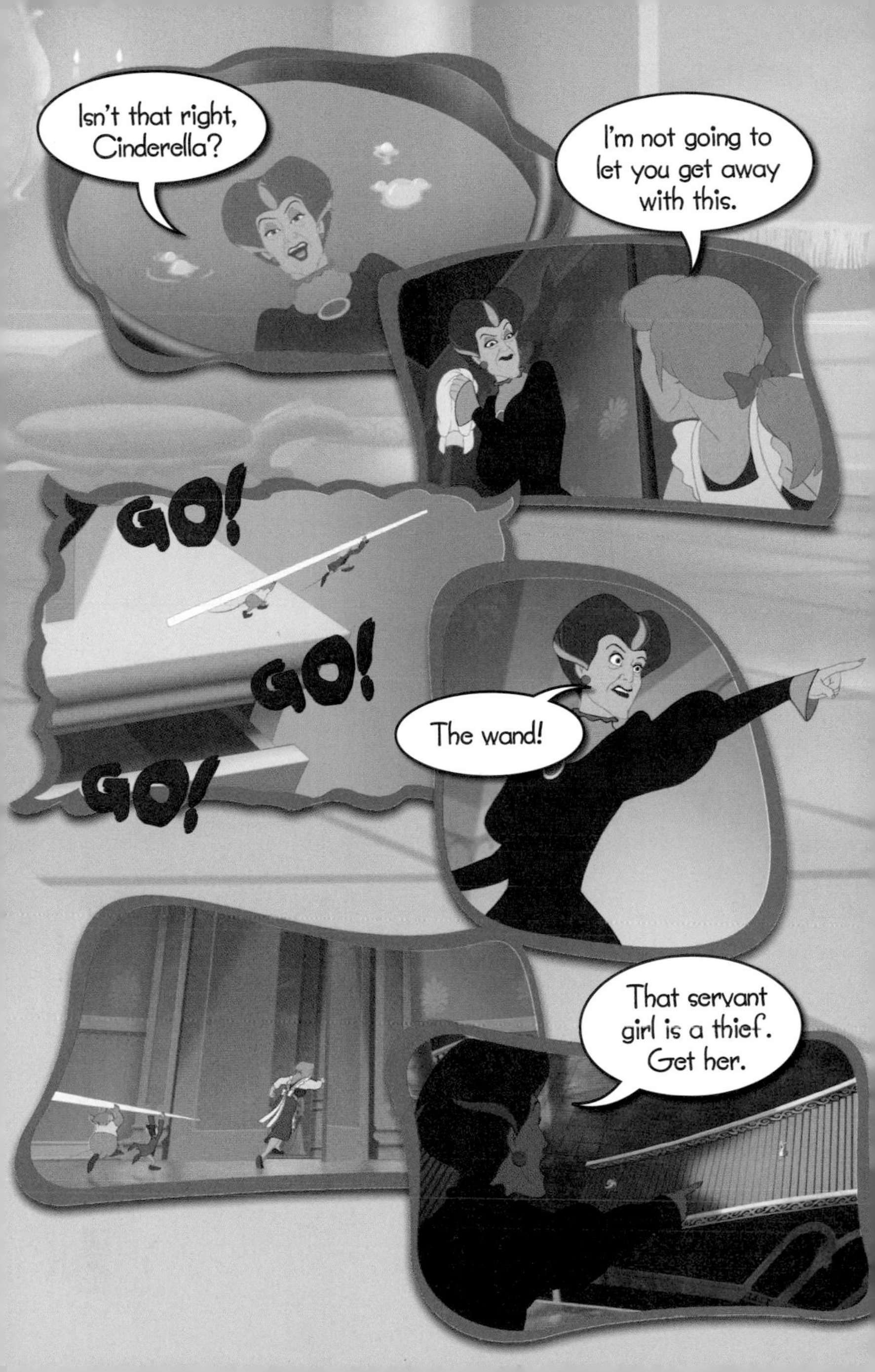
Isn't that right, Cinderella?
I'm not going to let you get away with this.
GO!
GO!
GO!
The wand!
That servant girl is a thief. Get her.

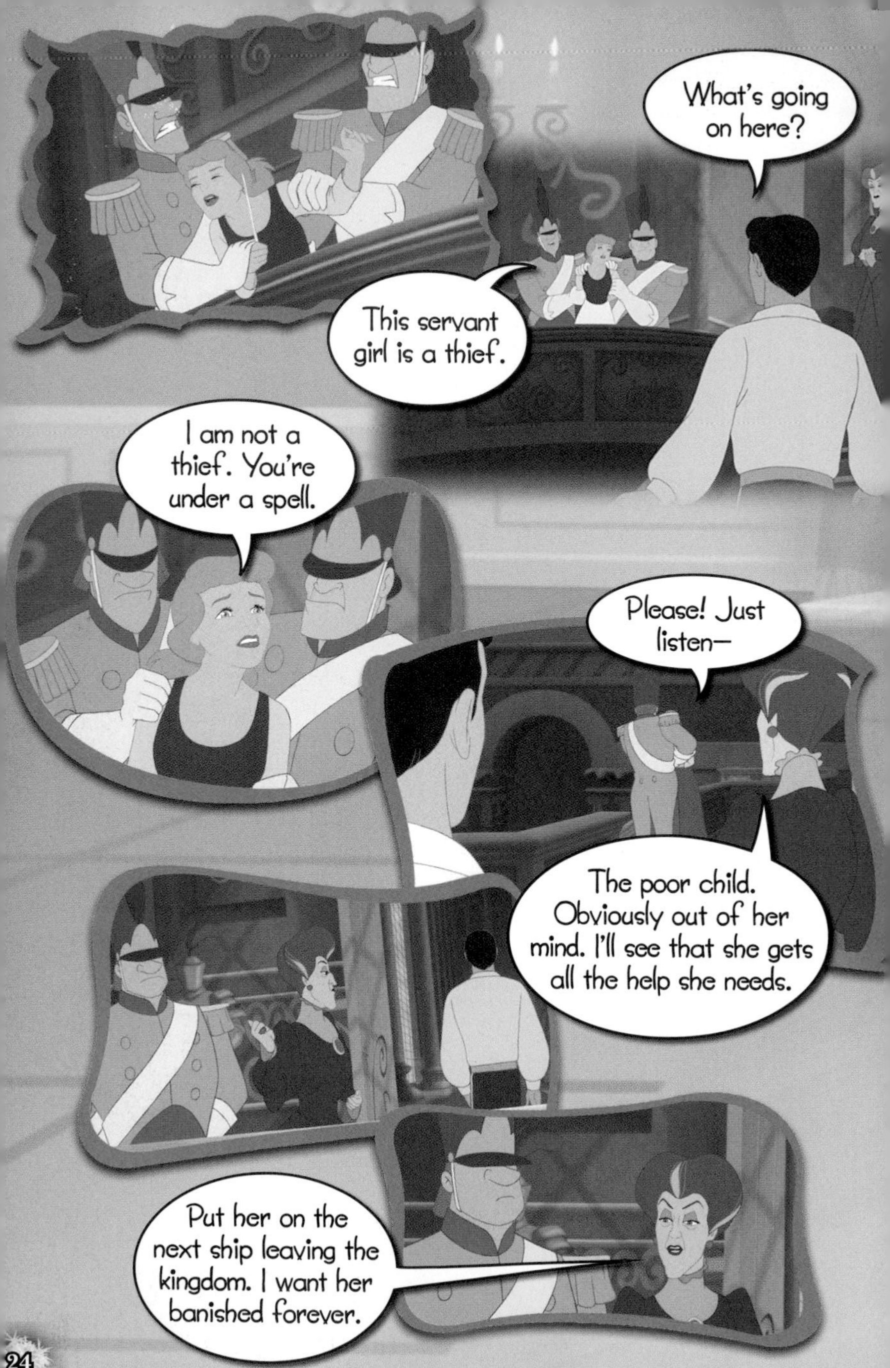
What's going on here?
This servant girl is a thief.
I am not a thief. You're under a spell.
Please! Just listen—
The poor child. Obviously out of her mind. I'll see that she gets all the help she needs.
Put her on the next ship leaving the kingdom. I want her banished forever.

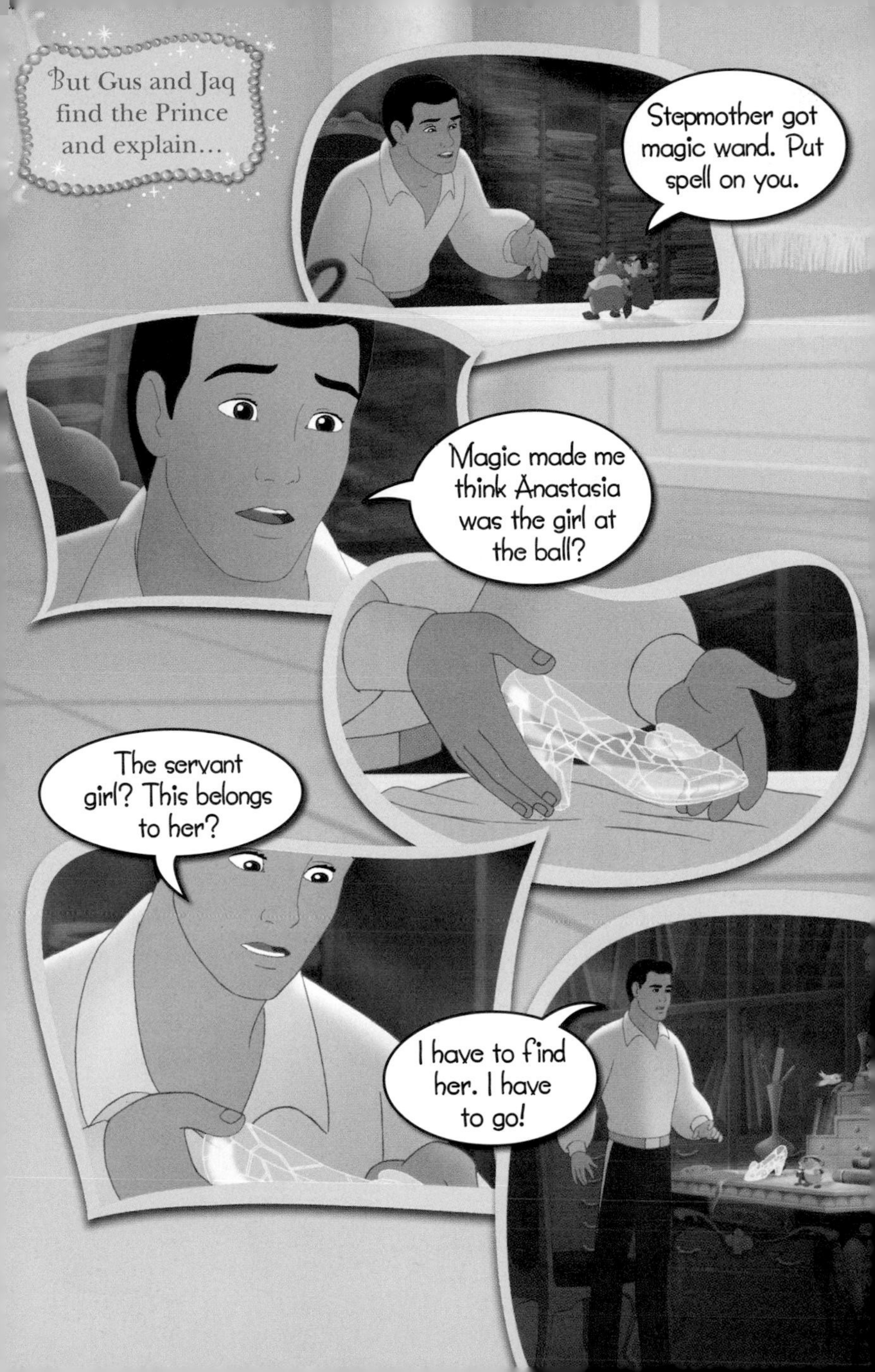
But Gus and Jaq find the Prince and explain...
Stepmother got magic wand. Put spell on you.
Magic made me think Anastasia was the girl at the ball?
The servant girl? This belongs to her?
I have to find her. I have to go!

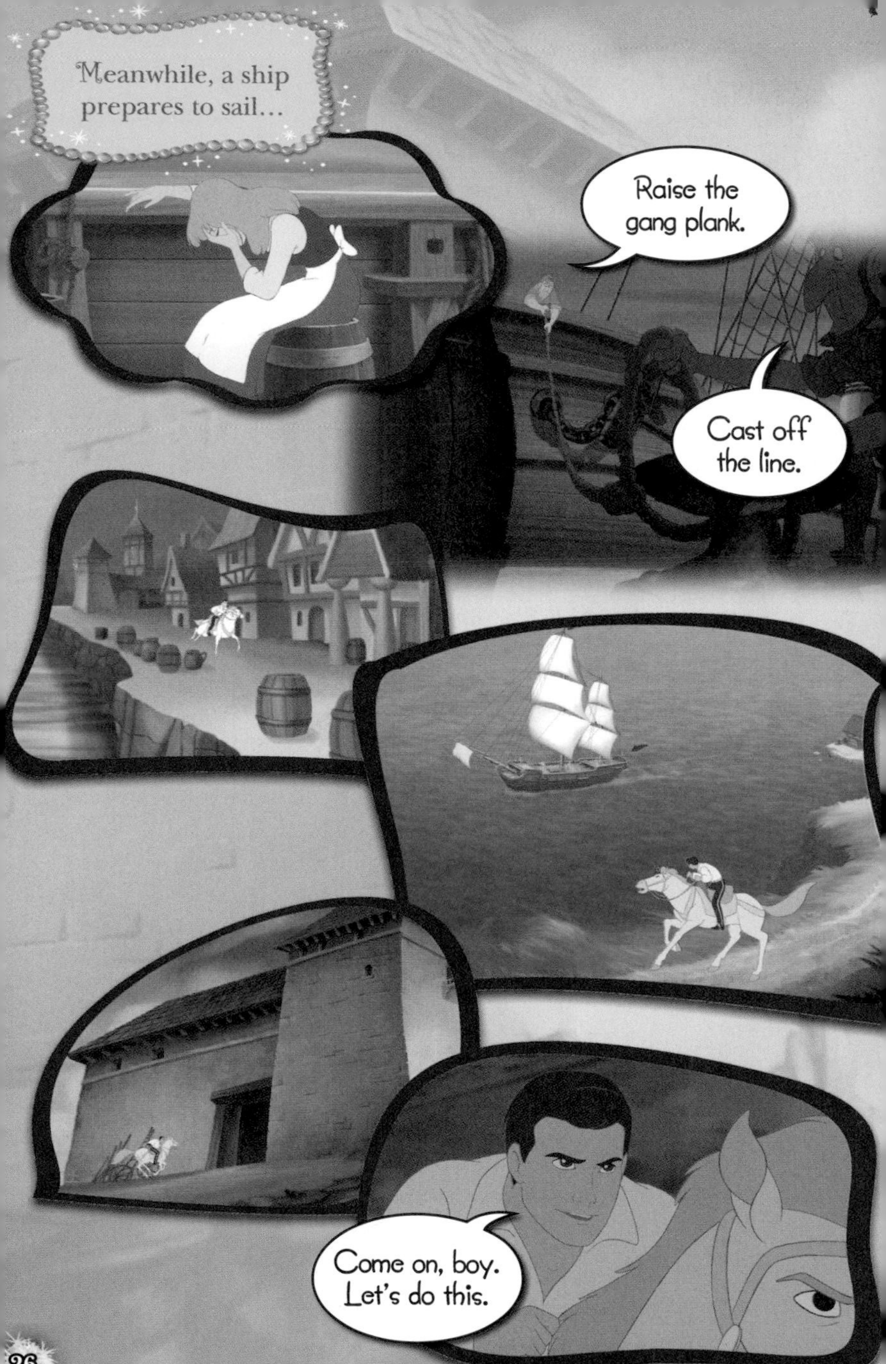
Meanwhile, a ship prepares to sail...
Raise the gang plank.
Cast off the line.
Come on, boy. Let's do this.

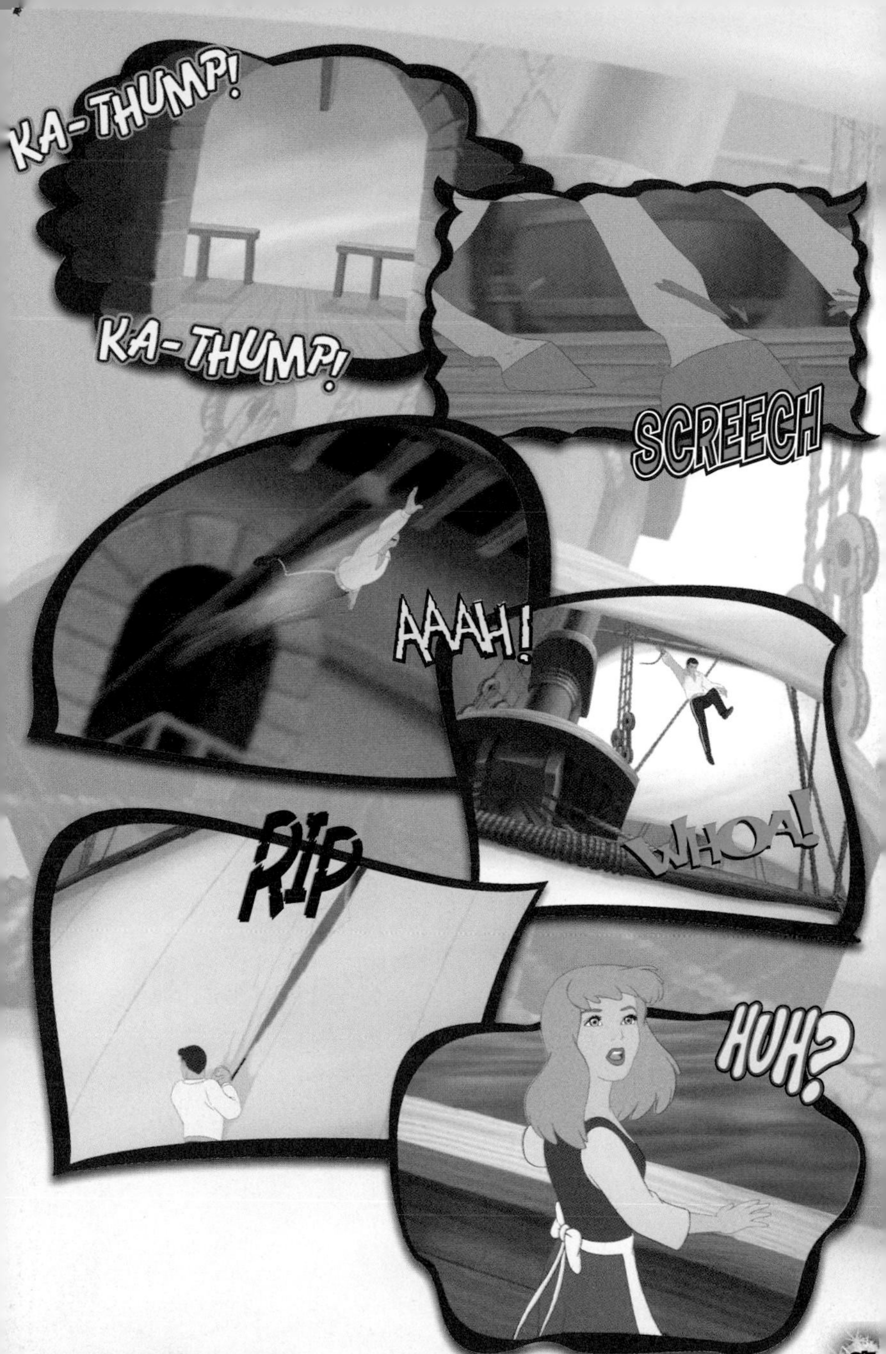
KA-THUMP!
KA-THUMP!
SCREECH
AAAH!
WHOA!
RIP
HUH?

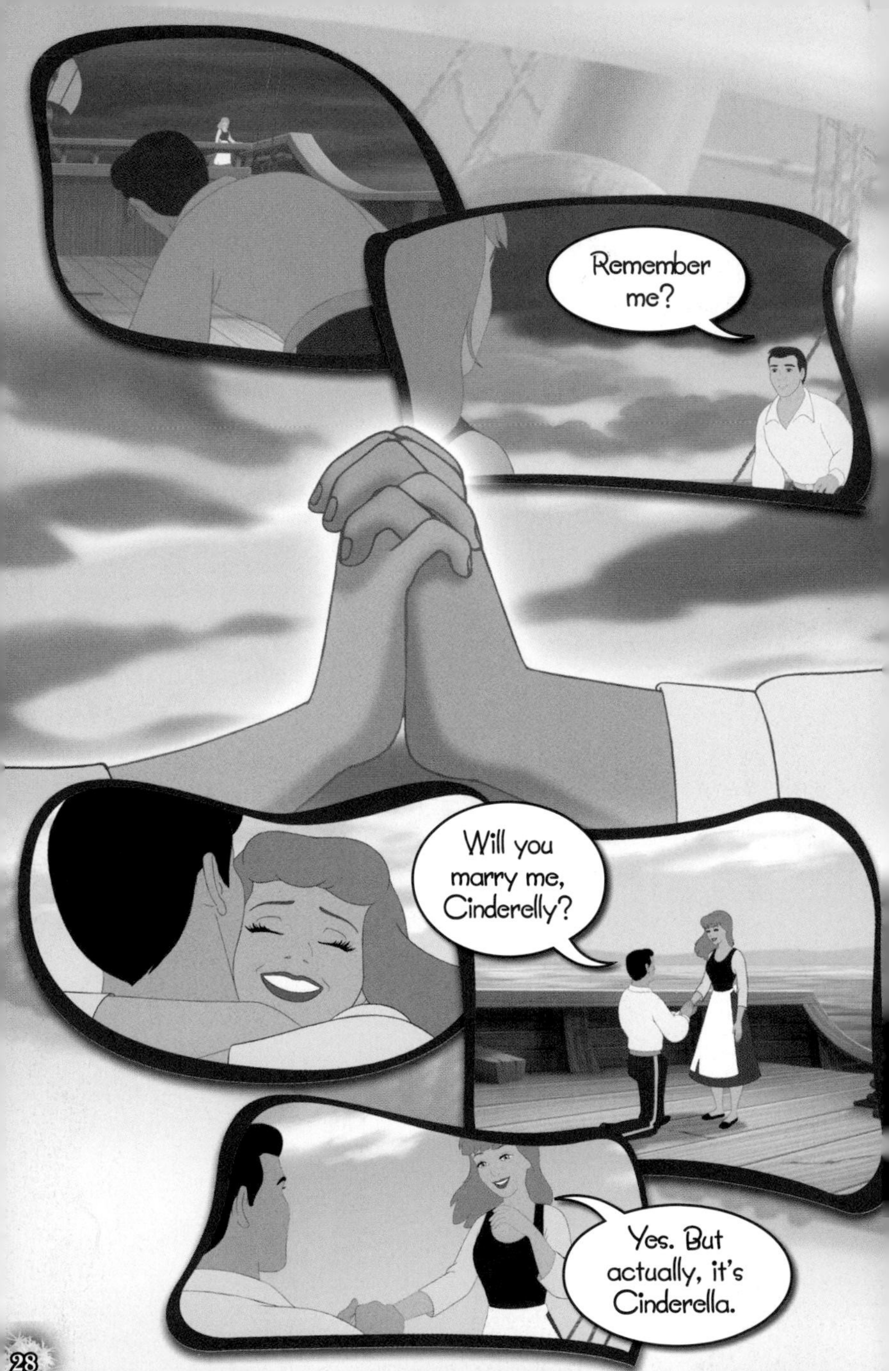
Remember me?
Will you marry me, Cinderelly?
Yes. But actually, it's Cinderella.

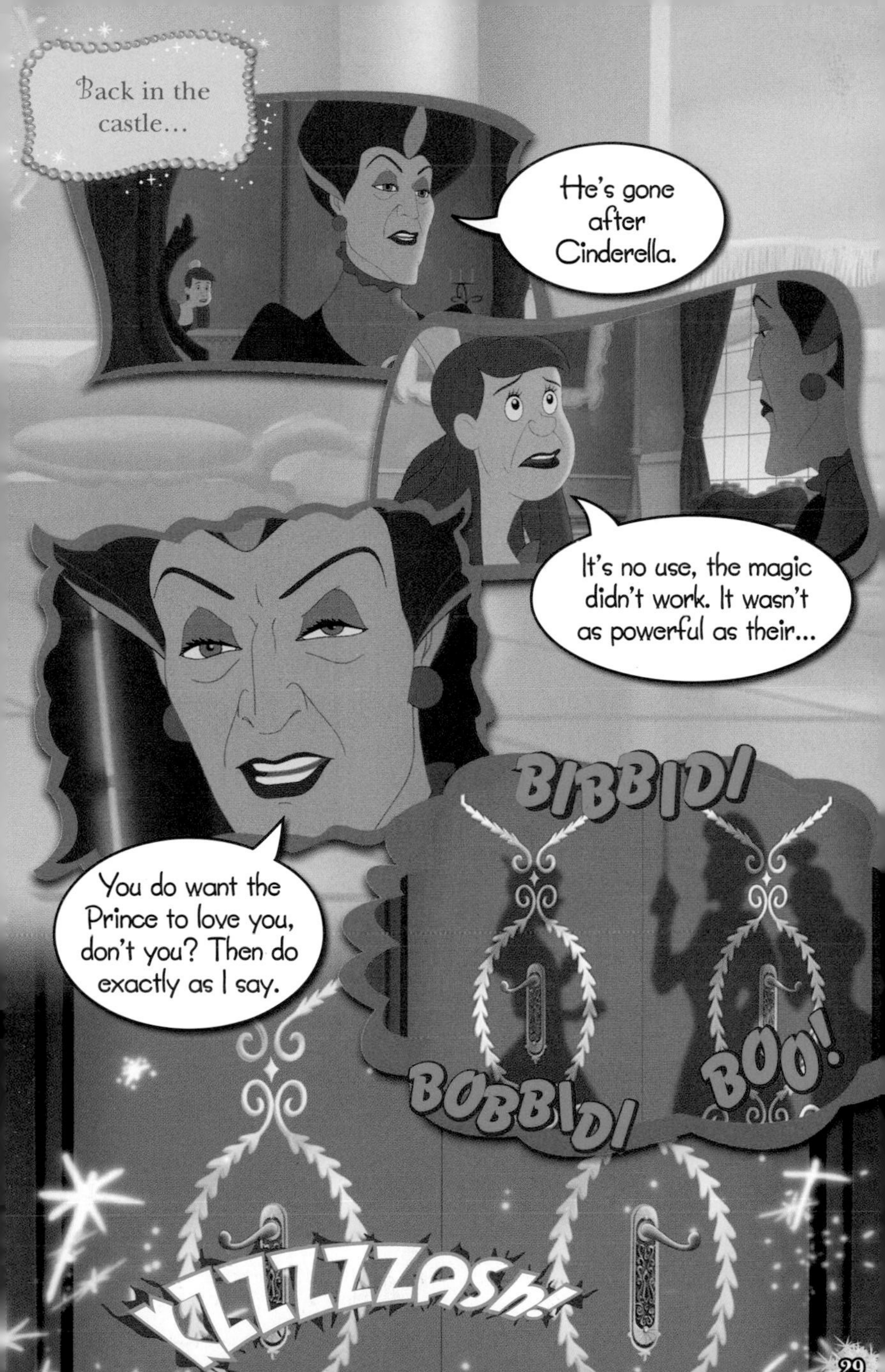
Back in the castle...
He's gone after Cinderella.
It's no use, the magic didn't work. It wasn't as powerful as their...
You do want the Prince to love you, don't you? Then do exactly as I say.
BIBBIDI
BOBBIDI
BOO!
KZZZZZZASH!

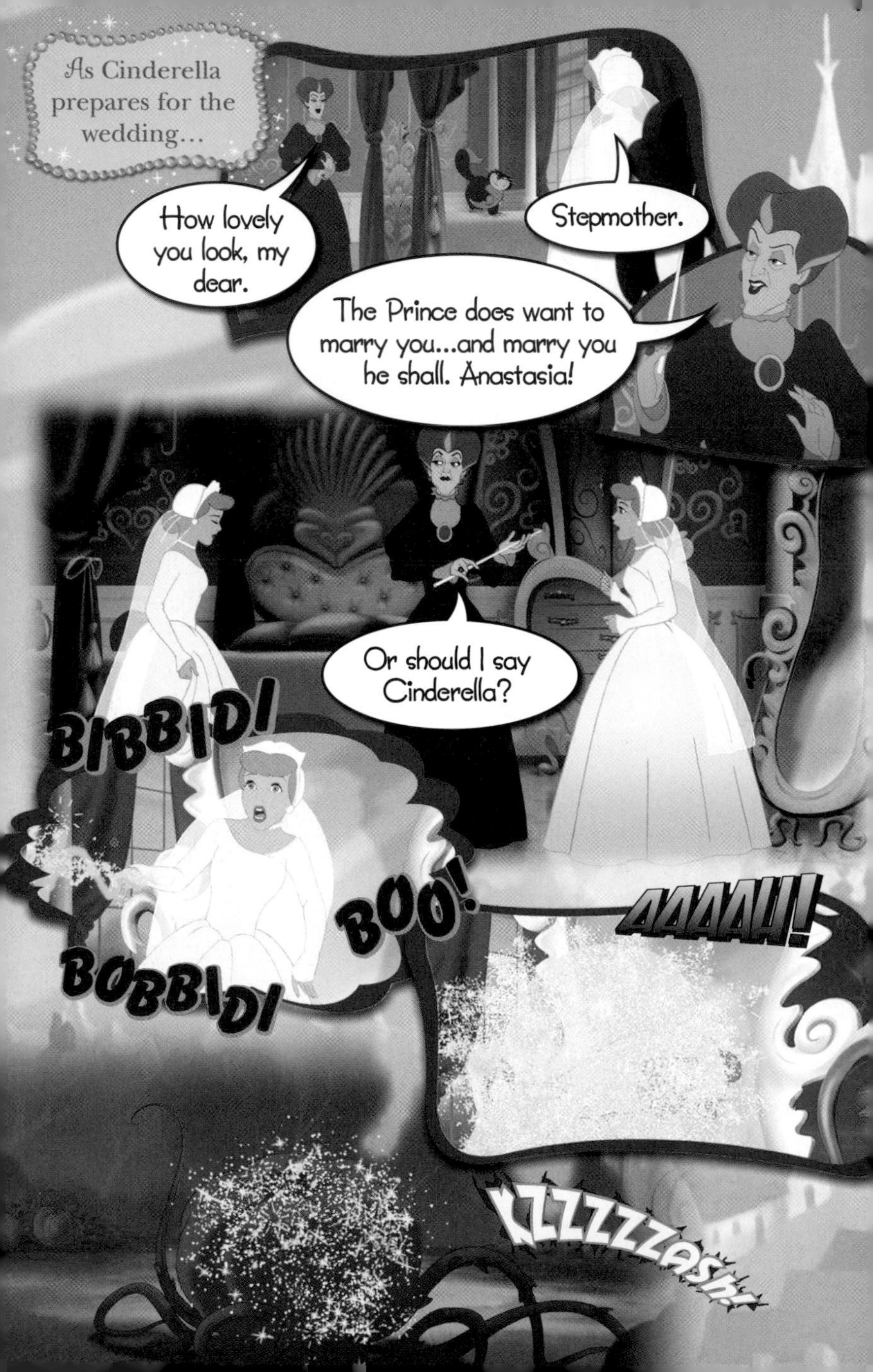
As Cinderella prepares for the wedding…
How lovely you look, my dear.
Stepmother.
The Prince does want to marry you...and marry you he shall. Anastasia!
Or should I say Cinderella?
BIBBIDI
BOBBIDI
BOO!
AAAAH!
KZZZZZZASH!

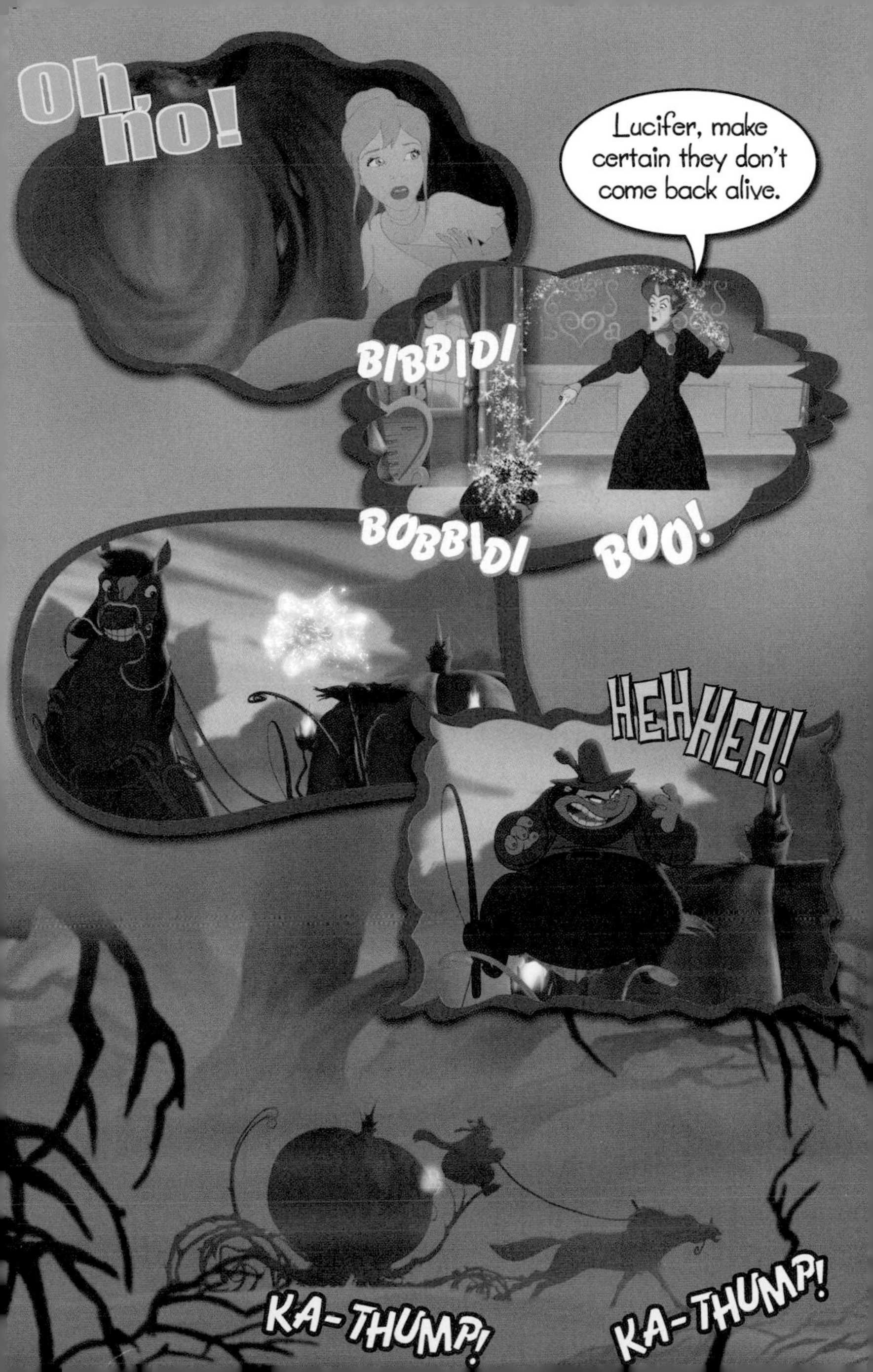

Oh, no!
Lucifer, make certain they don't come back alive.
BIBBIDI
BOBBIDI
BOO!
HEH HEH!
KA-THUMP!
KA-THUMP!

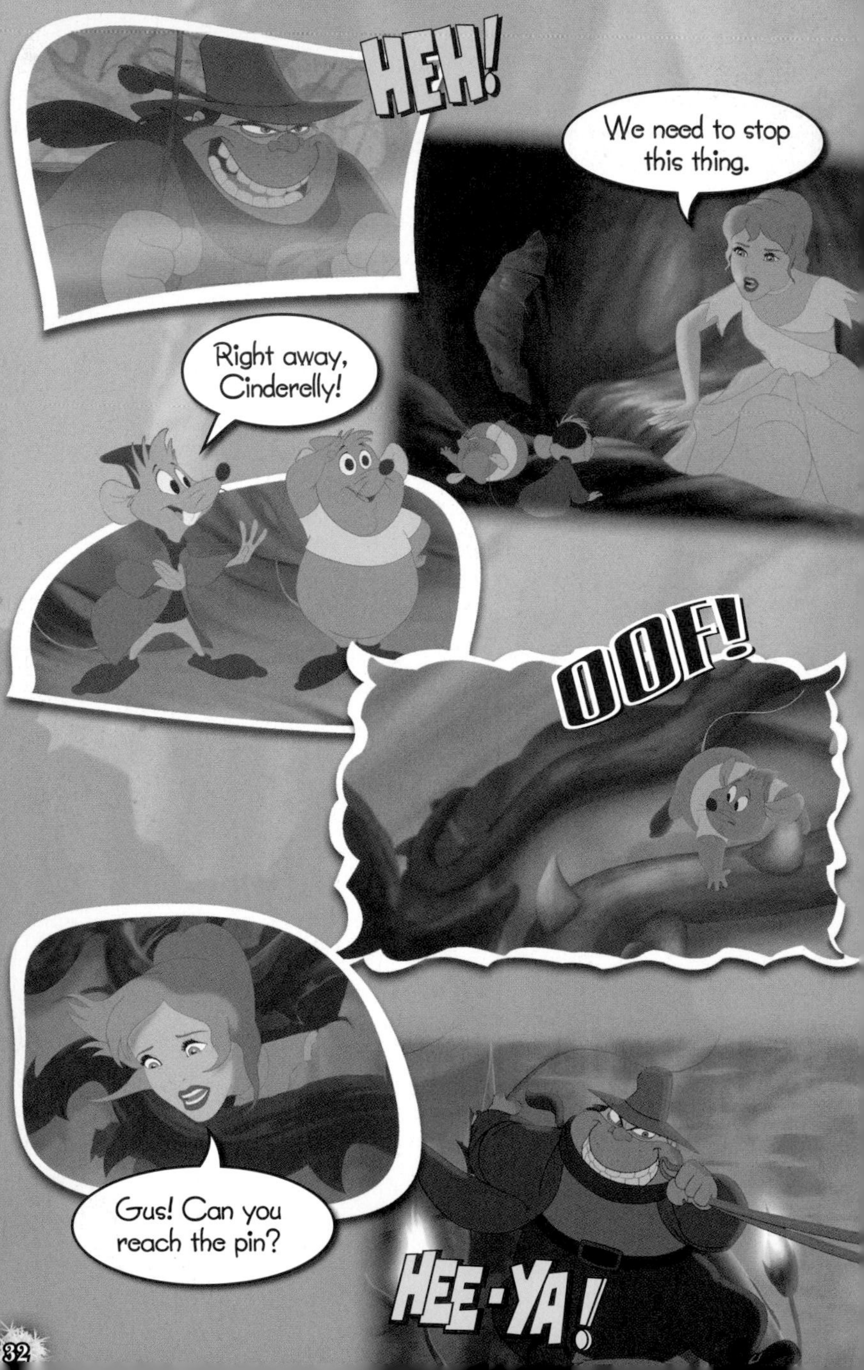
HEH!
We need to stop this thing.
Right away, Cinderelly!
OOF!
Gus! Can you reach the pin?
HEE-YA!

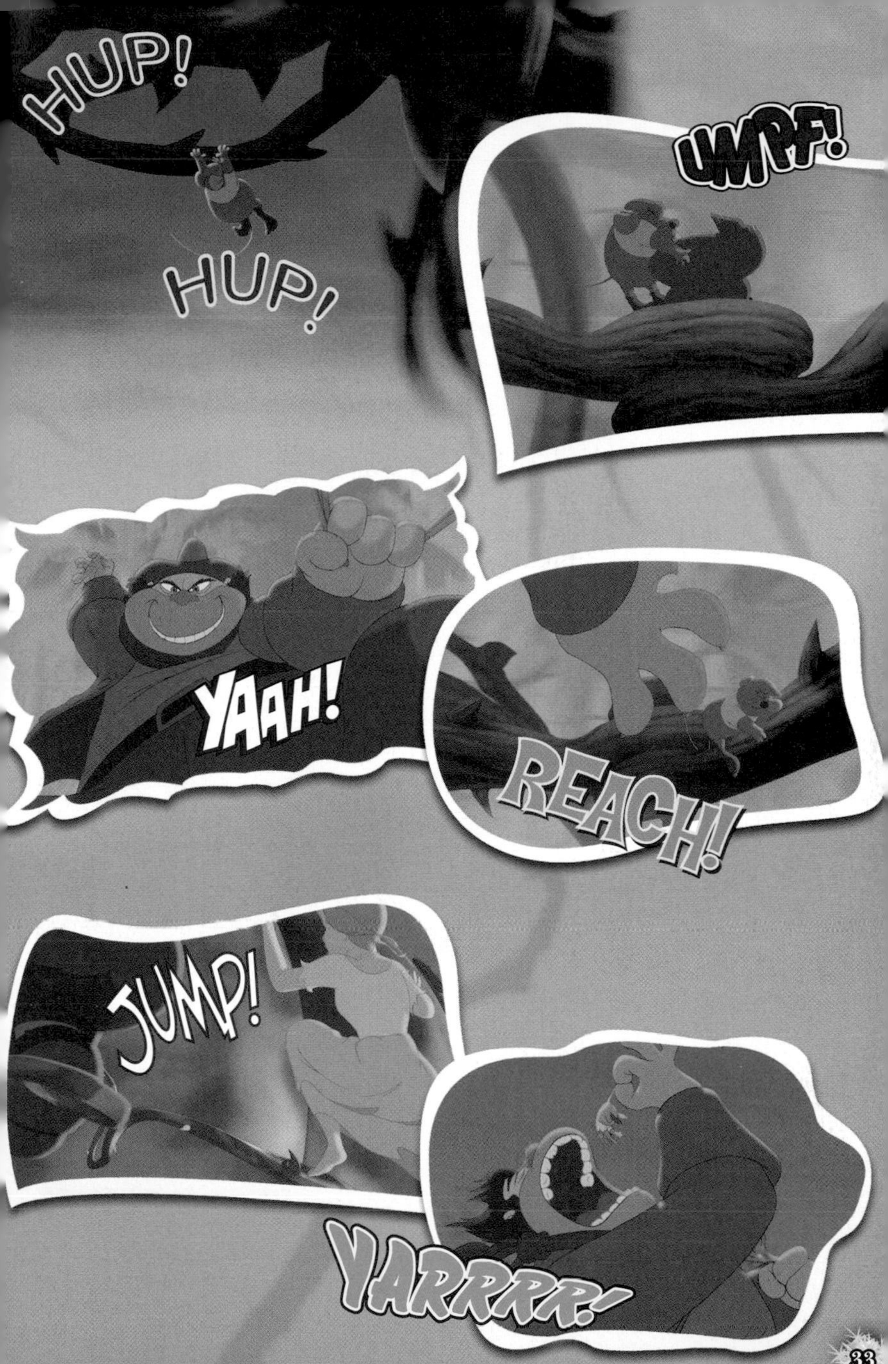
HUP!
HUP!
UMPF!
YAAH!
REACH!
JUMP!
YARRRR!

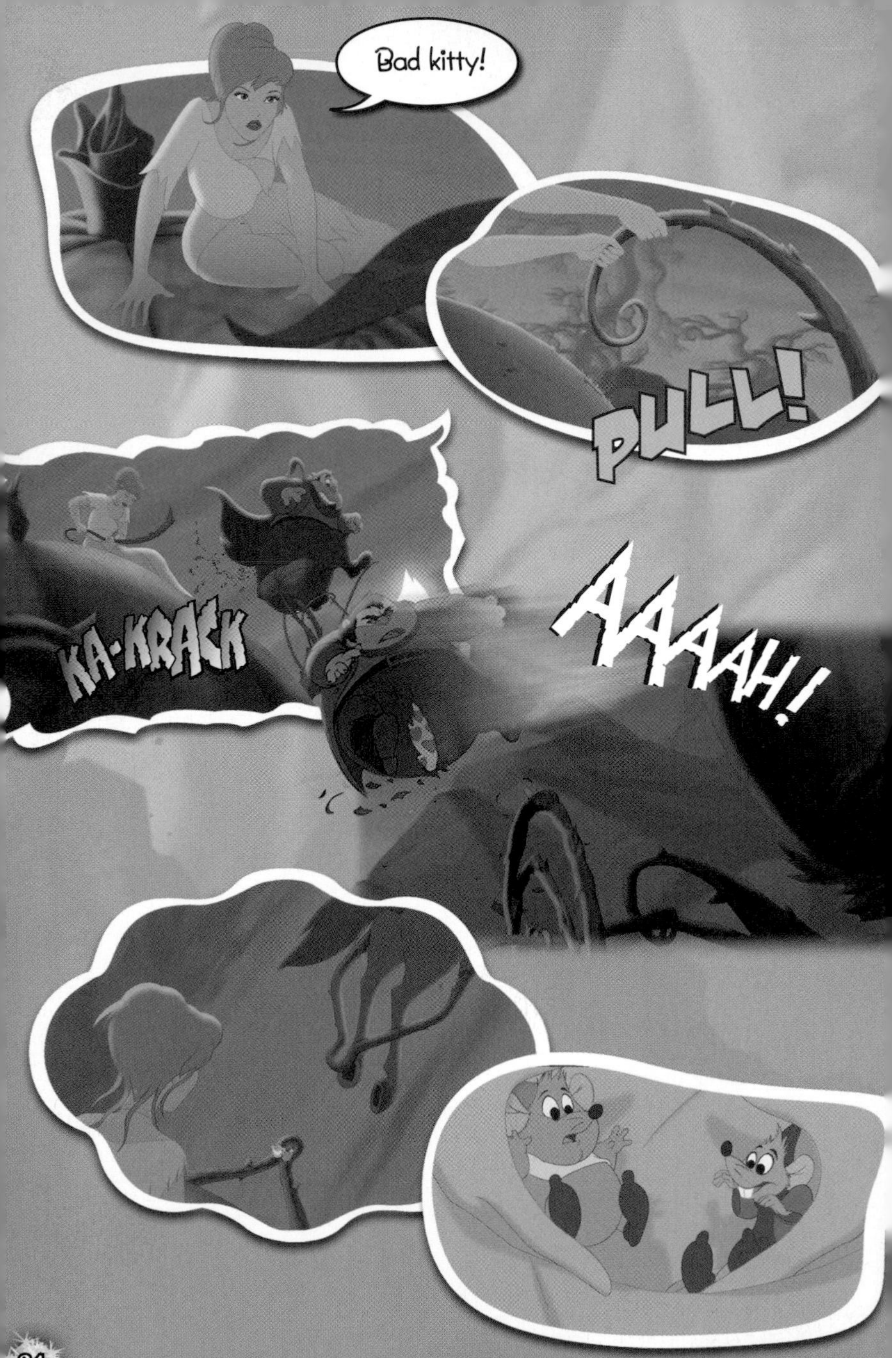
Bad kitty!
PULL!
KA-KRACK
AAAAH!

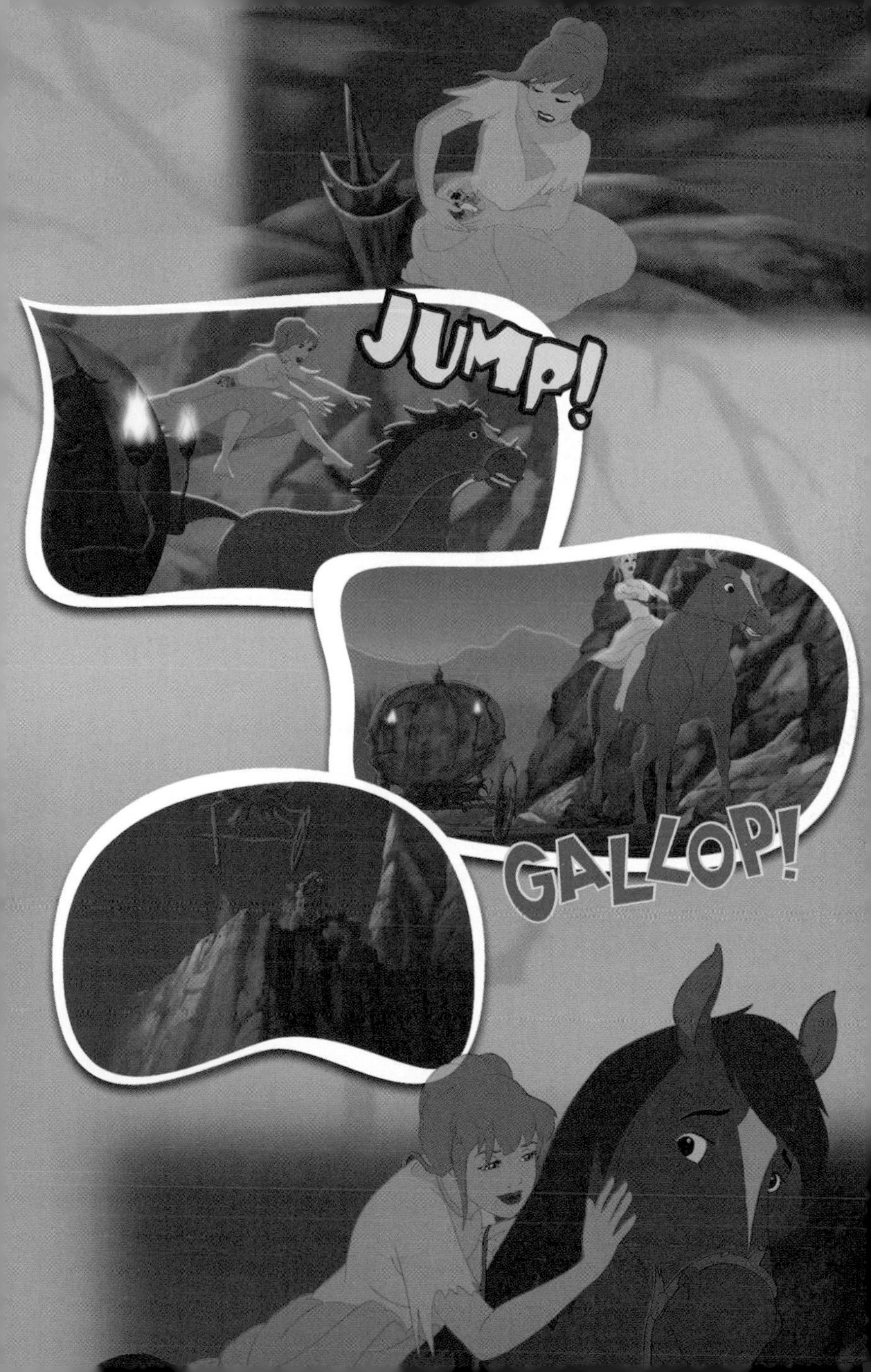
JUMP!
GALLOP!

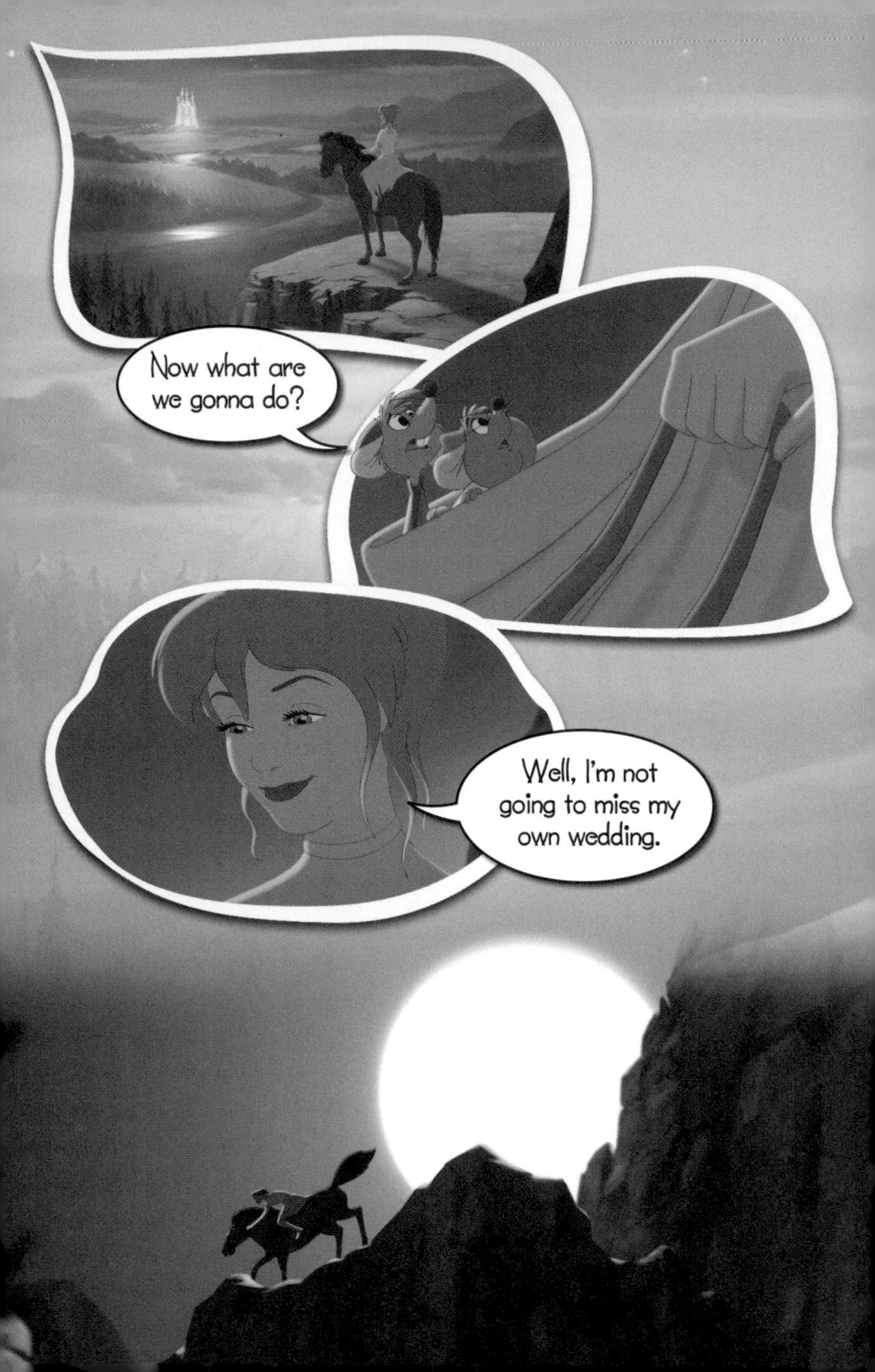
Now what are we gonna do?
Well, I'm not going to miss my own wedding.

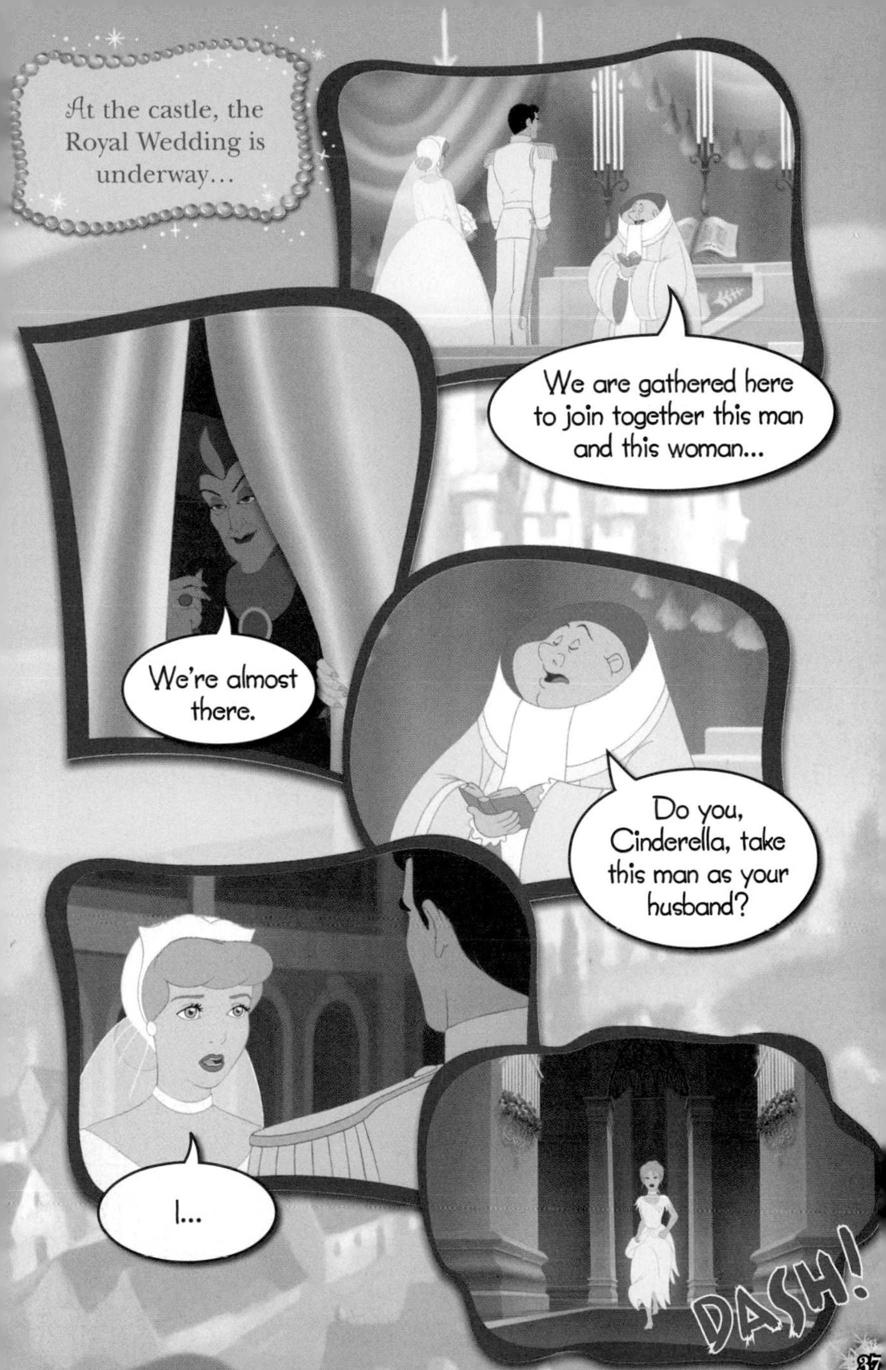
At the castle, the Royal Wedding is underway...
We are gathered here to join together this man and this woman...
We're almost there.
Do you, Cinderella, take this man as your husband?
I...
DASH!

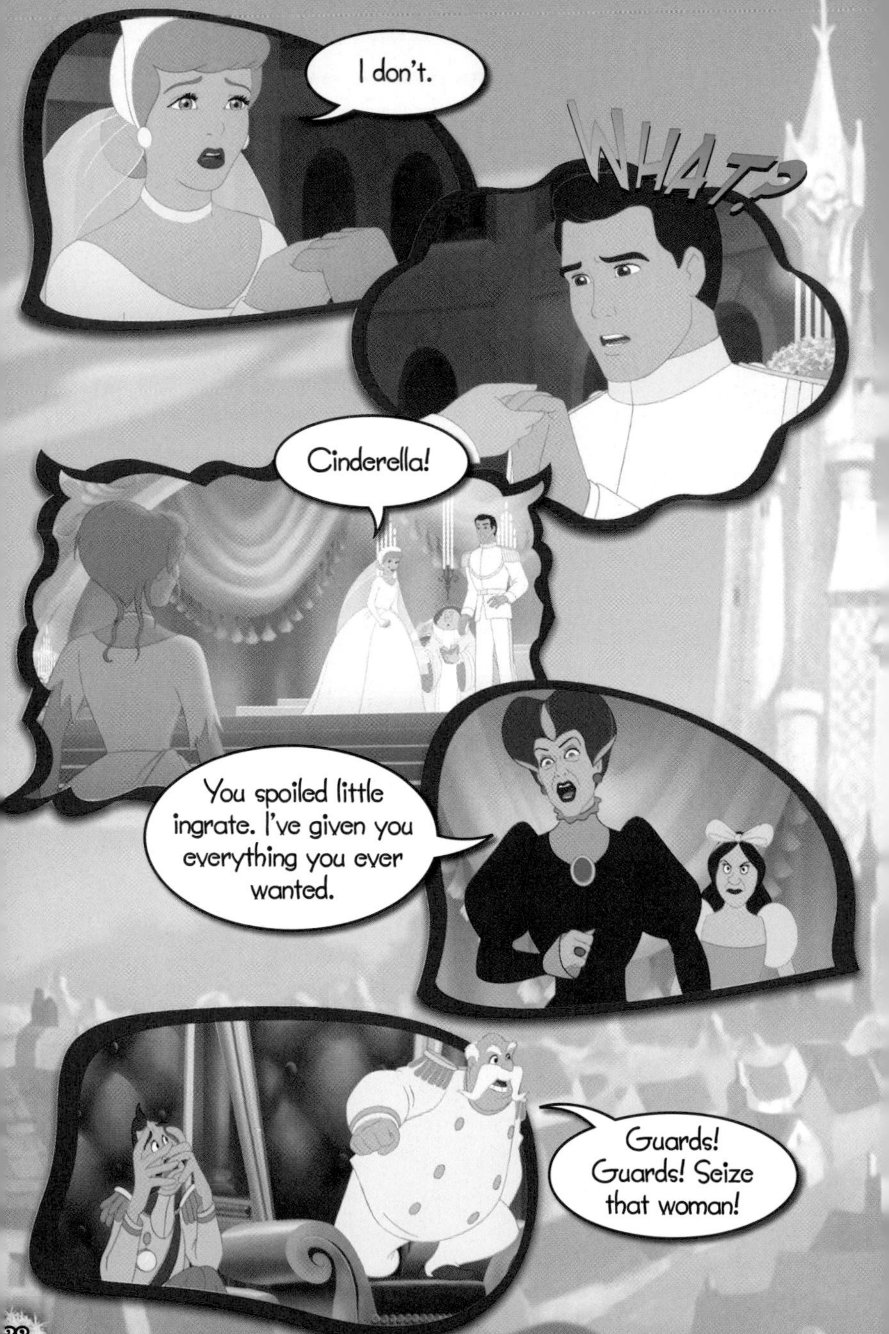
I don't.
WHAT?
Cinderella!
You spoiled little ingrate. I've given you everything you ever wanted.
Guards! Guards! Seize that woman!

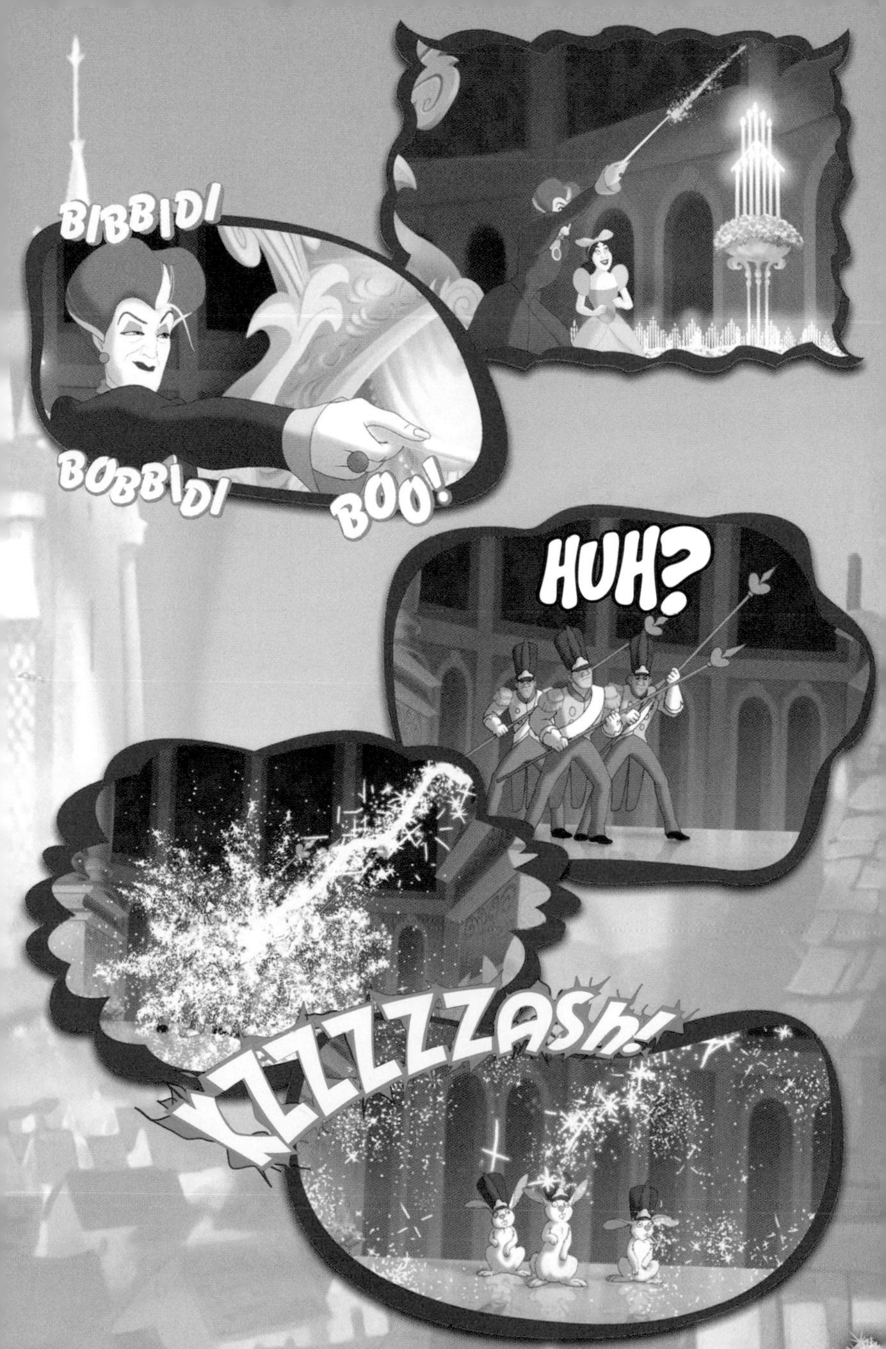
BIBBIDI
BOBBIDI
BOO!
HUH?
KZZZZZZASh!

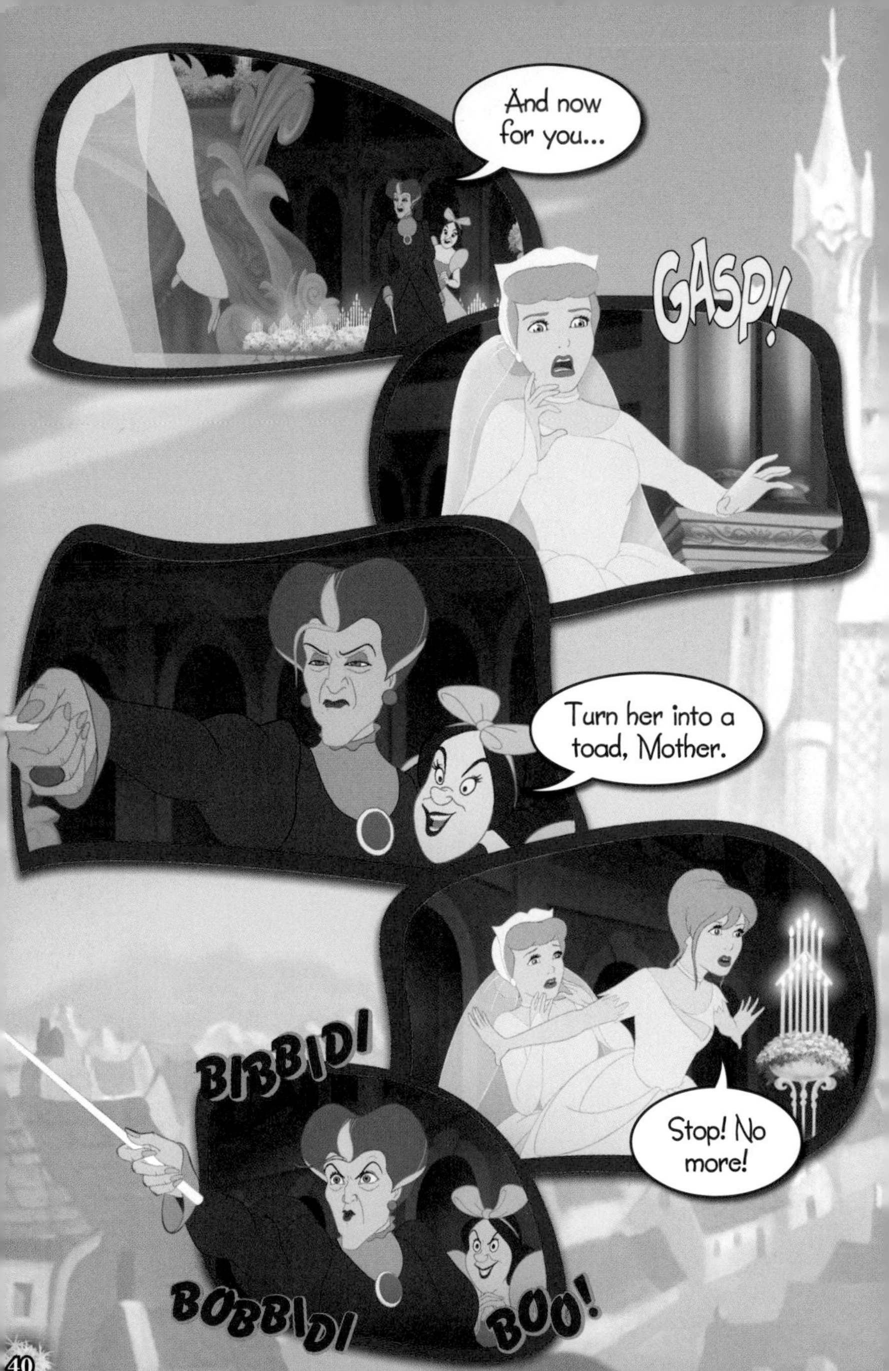
And now for you...
GASP!
Turn her into a toad, Mother.
Stop! No more!
BIBBIDI
BOBBIDI
BOO!

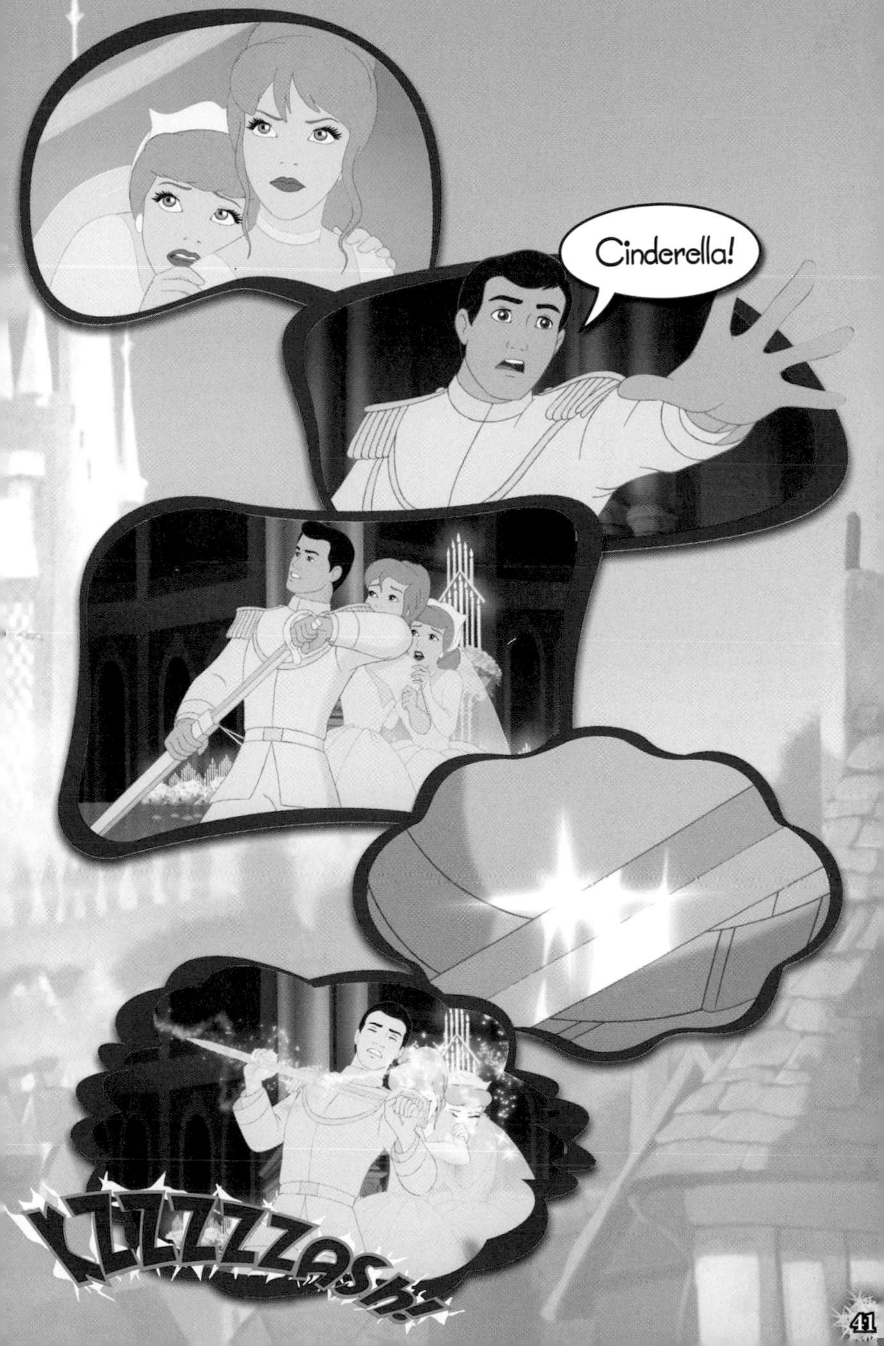
Cinderella!
KZZZZash!

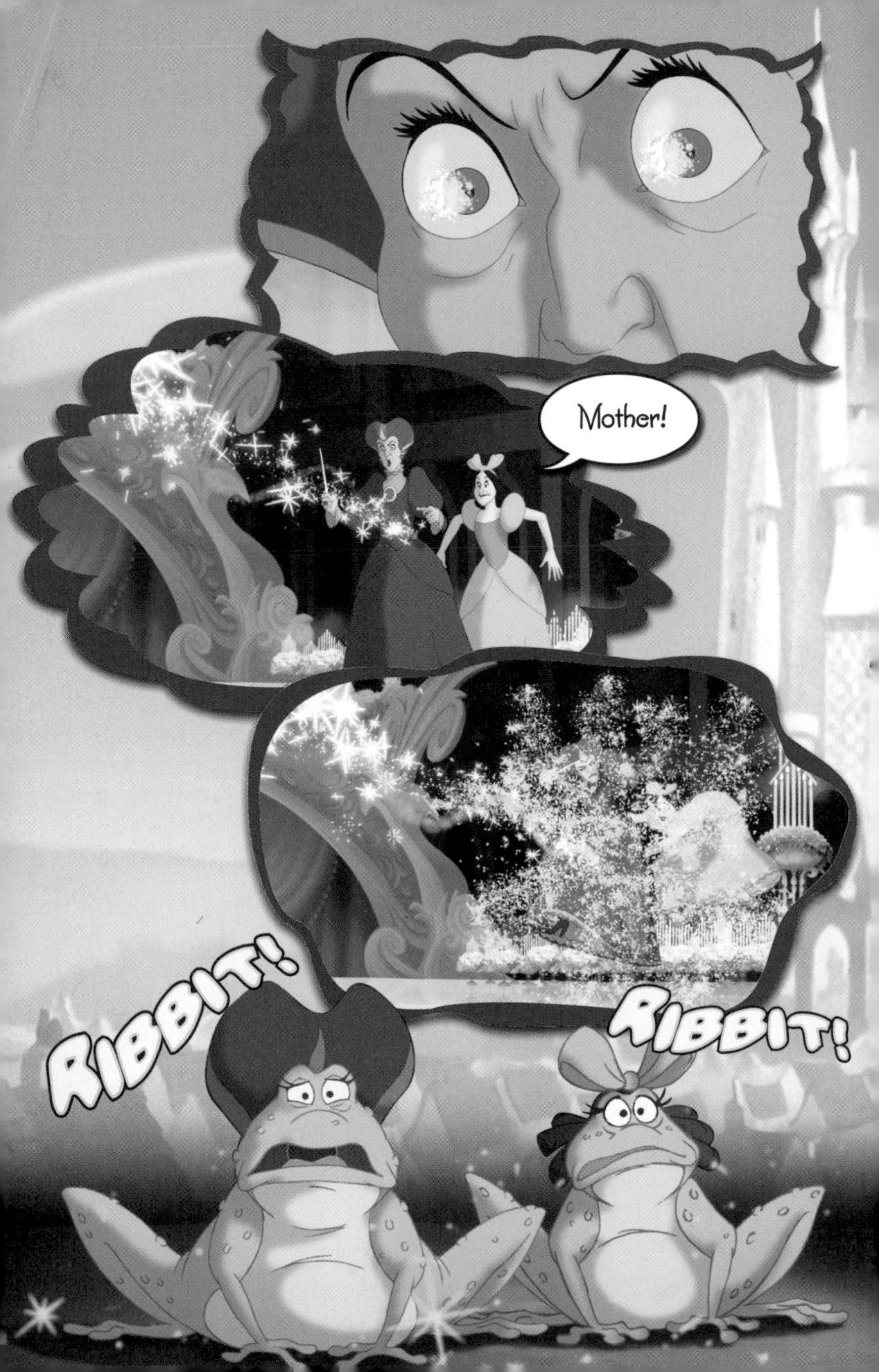
Mother!
RIBBIT!
RIBBIT!

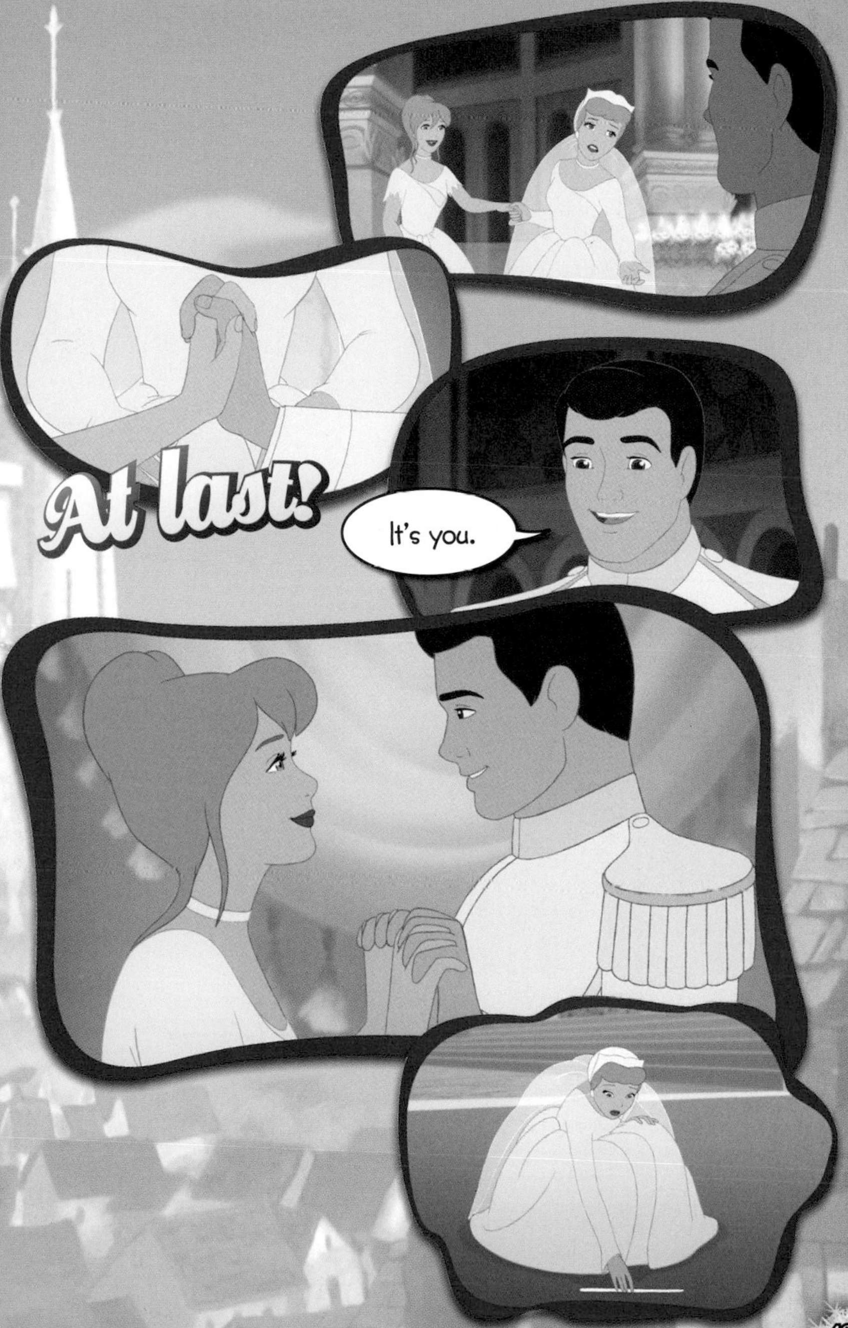
At last!
It's you.

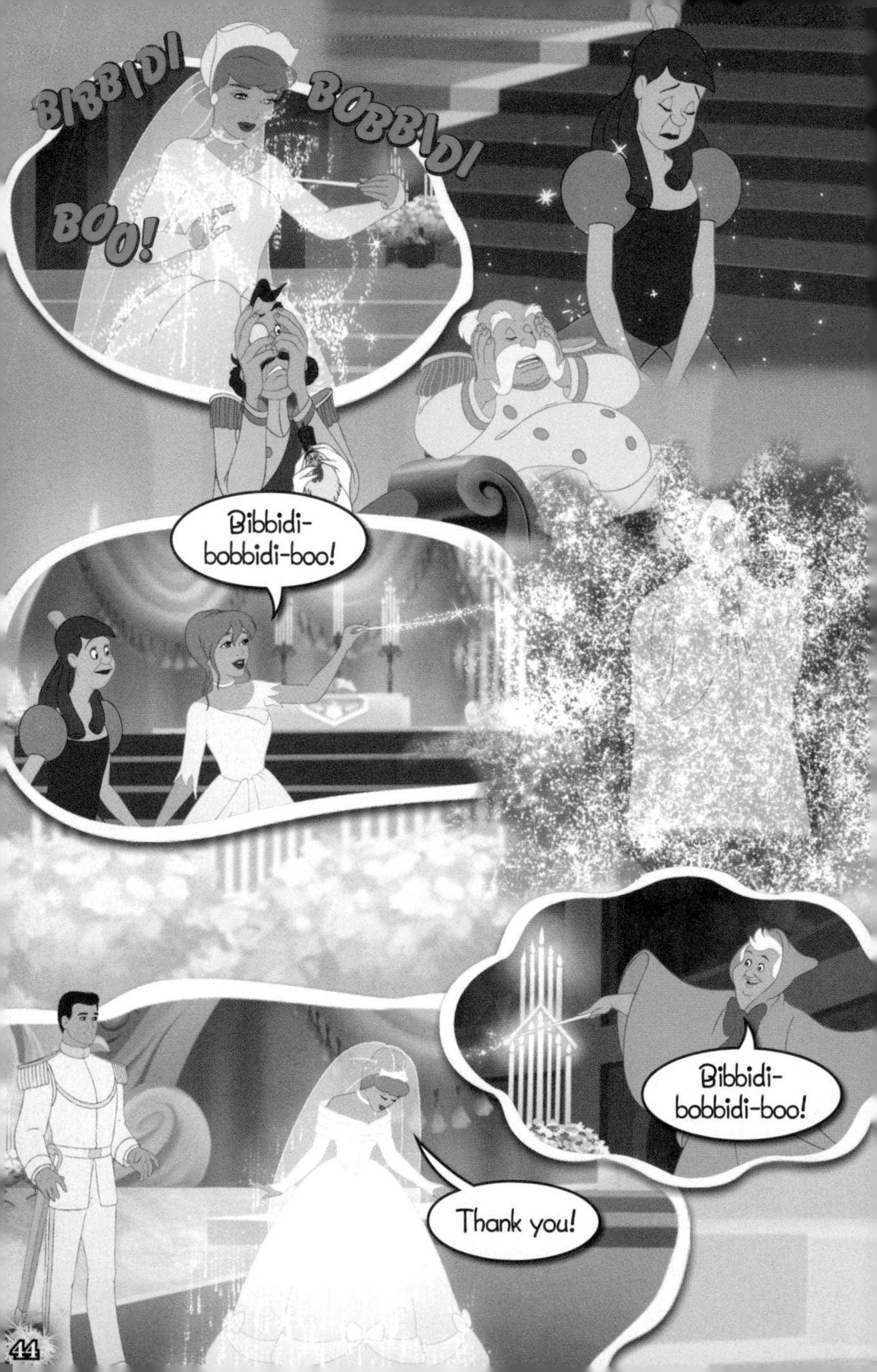
BIBBIDI
BOBBIDI
BOO!
Bibbidi-bobbidi-boo!
Bibbidi-bobbidi-boo!
Thank you!

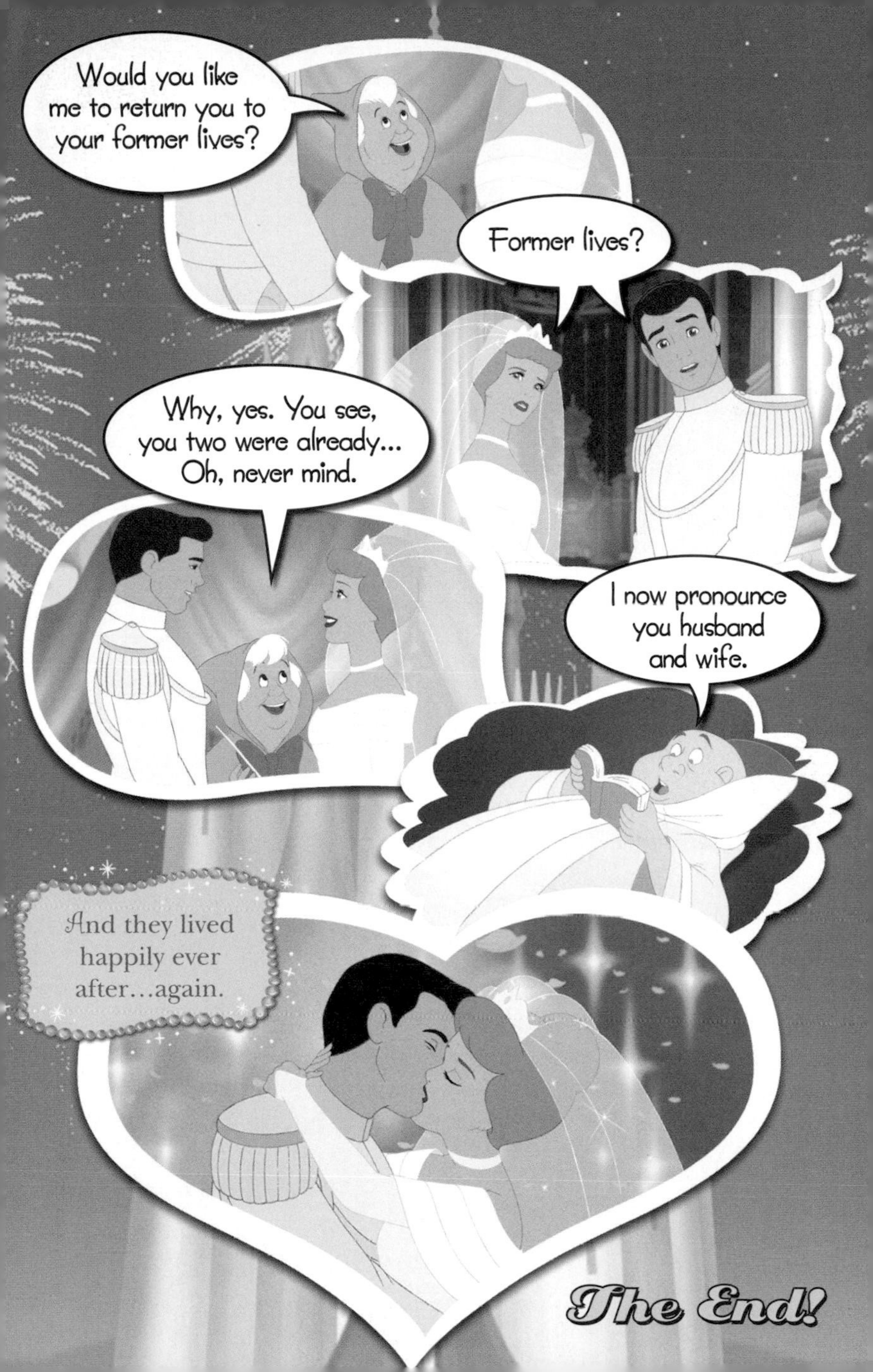
Would you like me to return you to your former lives?
Former lives?
Why, yes. You see, you two were already... Oh, never mind.
I now pronounce you husband and wife.
And they lived happily ever after…again.
The End!